JUMBLE® Parachute

Fall for These Thrilling Puzzles!

Henri Arnold,
Bob Lee,
Mike Argirion,
Jeff Knurek, &
David L. Hoyt

TRIUMPH
BOOKS

This book is available in quantity at special discounts
for your group or organization.

For further information, contact:

Triumph Books LLC
814 North Franklin Street
Chicago, Illinois 60610
Phone: (312) 337-0747
www.triumphbooks.com

Printed in U.S.A.

ISBN: 978-1-62937-548-9

Design by Sue Knopf

Contents

JUMBLE®

JUMBLE®
Parachute

Classic Puzzles

PUZZLE
1

JUMBLE®

Unscramble these four Jumbles, one letter to each square, to form four ordinary words.

BROAN

TEALE

TARPET

MORFIN

Let's get out of here!
ONE WAY TO BE A FOOL.

Now arrange the circled letters to form the surprise answer, as suggested by the above cartoon.

Print answer here ◯◯◯◯ WITH ◯ ◯◯◯

PUZZLE
2

JUMBLE®

Unscramble these four Jumbles, one letter to each square, to form four ordinary words.

CAPNI
SWOHE
TANQUI
REEWKS
How does he do it?
HOW TO FIND OUT A TIGHTROPE WALKER'S SECRET.

Now arrange the circled letters to form the surprise answer, as suggested by the above cartoon.

Print answer here

PUZZLE
3

JUMBLE®

Unscramble these four Jumbles, one letter to each square, to form four ordinary words.

TURET

RAOAM

AHNRAG

GOLLAB

Now you're all deputies
We'll get 'em, Sheriff
WHAT THE GUYS WHO STOLE THE SHEEP WERE.

Now arrange the circled letters to form the surprise answer, as suggested by the above cartoon.

Print answer here ⃝⃝ ⃝⃝⃝ "⃝⃝⃝⃝"

PUZZLE
4

JUMBLE®

Unscramble these four Jumbles, one letter to each square, to form four ordinary words.

YATTS
IKKAH
SMALID
FAINAR
WHAT THEY CALLED THE PARAMEDICS' MASCOT.
Print answer here THE ______-___ "___"

Now arrange the circled letters to form the surprise answer, as suggested by the above cartoon.

PUZZLE
5

JUMBLE®

Unscramble these four Jumbles, one letter to each square, to form four ordinary words.

NESOO
YARPT
ANZATS
INFISH
Sorry I'm late, dear
THE POINT ABOUT THIS IS THAT IT'S KEPT HIDDEN.

Now arrange the circled letters to form the surprise answer, as suggested by the above cartoon.

Print answer here A

PUZZLE
6

JUMBLE®

Unscramble these four Jumbles, one letter to each square, to form four ordinary words.

SWENY
CUNDE
BEMDOY
INTOUG
IF THE BRIDE LOOKED STUNNING, HOW DID THE GROOM LOOK?

Now arrange the circled letters to form the surprise answer, as suggested by the above cartoon.

Print answer here

PUZZLE
7

JUMBLE®

Unscramble these four Jumbles, one letter to each square, to form four ordinary words.

VEVER

REHKI

ENTAIN

COMTIA

THEY MIGHT BE SHOWN WITH A SMILE.

Now arrange the circled letters to form the surprise answer, as suggested by the above cartoon.

Print answer here

PUZZLE
8

JUMBLE®

Unscramble these four Jumbles, one letter to each square, to form four ordinary words.

SUMOY
RADOH
AKCEPT
YARQUR
A TRICK THAT TAKES US IN.

Now arrange the circled letters to form the surprise answer, as suggested by the above cartoon.

Print answer here ☐ "☐-☐☐-☐"

PUZZLE
9

JUMBLE®

Unscramble these four Jumbles, one letter to each square, to form four ordinary words.

WEPOR

NIGTY

VERROF

PANPHE

DISCO
BY THE TIME A MAN IS WISE ENOUGH TO WATCH HIS STEP, HE'S USUALLY TOO OLD TO DO THIS.

Now arrange the circled letters to form the surprise answer, as suggested by the above cartoon.

Print answer here

PUZZLE
10

JUMBLE®

Unscramble these four Jumbles, one letter to each square, to form four ordinary words.

SAYGS
THERB
SNELET
CAFEED
$
FURS
A SOFT TOUCH.

Now arrange the circled letters to form the surprise answer, as suggested by the above cartoon.

Print answer here A

PUZZLE
11

JUMBLE®

Unscramble these four Jumbles, one letter to each square, to form four ordinary words.

KAYWG
NIROY
LESTUS
DAYNIT
THE SAILOR TURNED MINISTER WAS SKILLED AT THIS.
Print answer here

Now arrange the circled letters to form the surprise answer, as suggested by the above cartoon.

PUZZLE
12

JUMBLE®

Unscramble these four Jumbles, one letter to each square, to form four ordinary words.

PRAVO
TILEE
HARTOX
RICHEP
IS IT GOING TO BE A LOCAL OR A GENERAL ANESTHETIC?

Now arrange the circled letters to form the surprise answer, as suggested by the above cartoon.

Print answer here "YOU CAN ◯◯◯◯ ◯◯◯◯◯"

PUZZLE
13

JUMBLE®

Unscramble these four Jumbles, one letter to each square, to form four ordinary words.

MOVEN
RABIR
GOUTIN
WHOALL
THE MINER DIDN'T KNOW WHETHER HE HAD STRUCK THIS.

Now arrange the circled letters to form the surprise answer, as suggested by the above cartoon.

Print answer here

PUZZLE
14

JUMBLE®

Unscramble these four Jumbles, one letter to each square, to form four ordinary words.

RUETT
CUEJI
DESSUR
JOADIN
WHAT THE LAWYER DEMANDED TO HAVE WITH HIS DRINK.

Now arrange the circled letters to form the surprise answer, as suggested by the above cartoon.

Print answer here " "

PUZZLE
15

JUMBLE®

Unscramble these four Jumbles, one letter to each square, to form four ordinary words.

MEPOT

CUNEL

WOTOWK

THANYS

WHO'S HEARD ABOUT THE BIG KIDNAPPING?

Now arrange the circled letters to form the surprise answer, as suggested by the above cartoon.

Print answer here " "

PUZZLE
16

JUMBLE®

Unscramble these four Jumbles, one letter to each square, to form four ordinary words.

RAYIF
NEEYM
RUPPEA
ALLTOW
WHAT THE RAM SAID TO THE FEMALE OF THE SPECIES.

Now arrange the circled letters to form the surprise answer, as suggested by the above cartoon.

Print answer here

PUZZLE
17

JUMBLE®

Unscramble these four Jumbles, one letter to each square, to form four ordinary words.

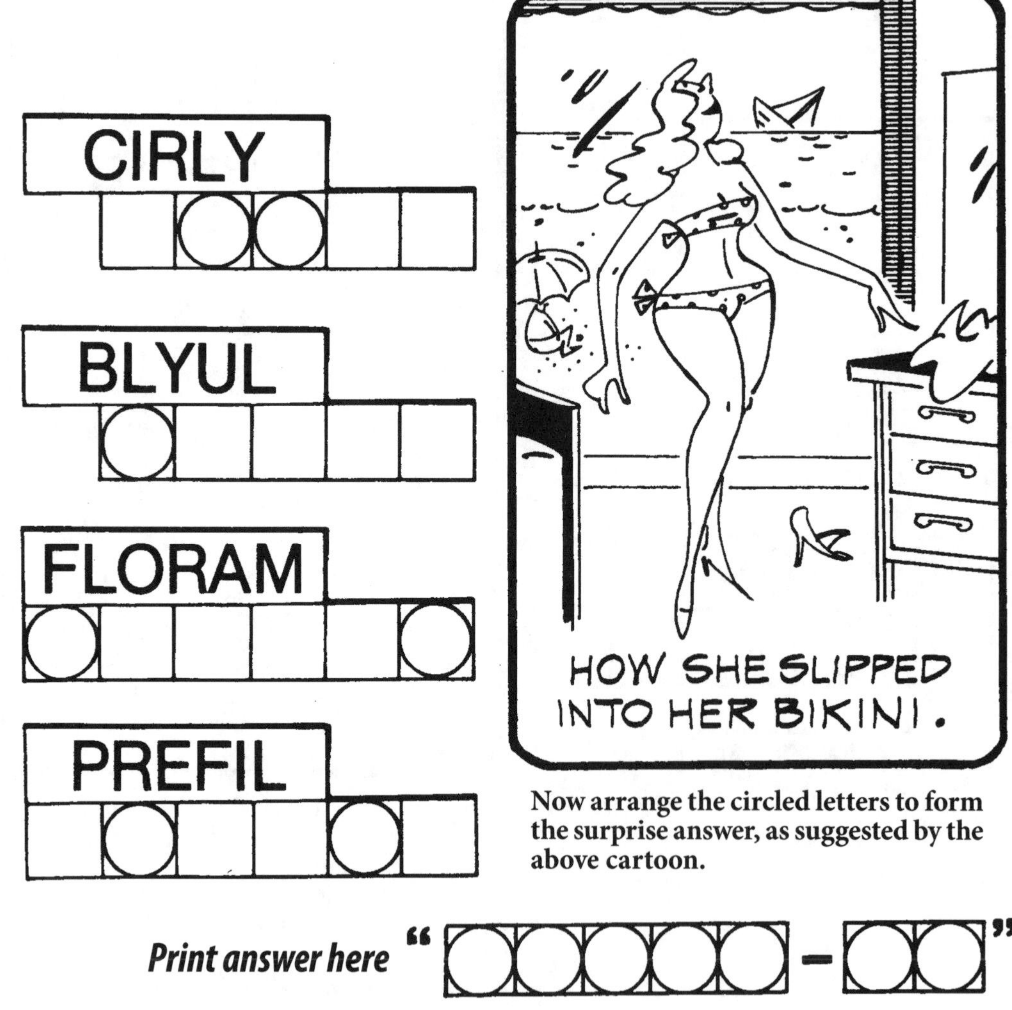
CIRLY
BLYUL
FLORAM
PREFIL
HOW SHE SLIPPED INTO HER BIKINI.

Now arrange the circled letters to form the surprise answer, as suggested by the above cartoon.

Print answer here "◯◯◯◯◯-◯◯"

PUZZLE
18

JUMBLE®

Unscramble these four Jumbles, one letter to each square, to form four ordinary words.

SNUKK
CEHOP
STUBOE
PASHIM
DELIVERY
1... 2... 3...
WHAT THE NEW FATHER OF QUINTU-PLETS JUST COULDN'T BELIEVE.
Print answer here
“ ”

Now arrange the circled letters to form the surprise answer, as suggested by the above cartoon.

PUZZLE
19

JUMBLE®

Unscramble these four Jumbles, one letter to each square, to form four ordinary words.

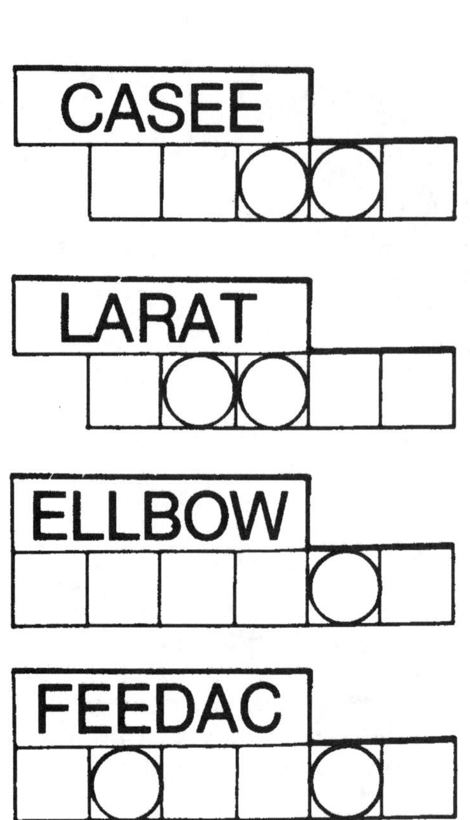
CASEE
LARAT
ELLBOW
FEEDAC

THE CROOKED ARCHI-
TECT DISCOVERED THAT
PRISON WALLS WEREN'T
BUILT THIS WAY.

Now arrange the circled letters to form the surprise answer, as suggested by the above cartoon.

Print answer here

PUZZLE
20

JUMBLE®

Unscramble these four Jumbles, one letter to each square, to form four ordinary words.

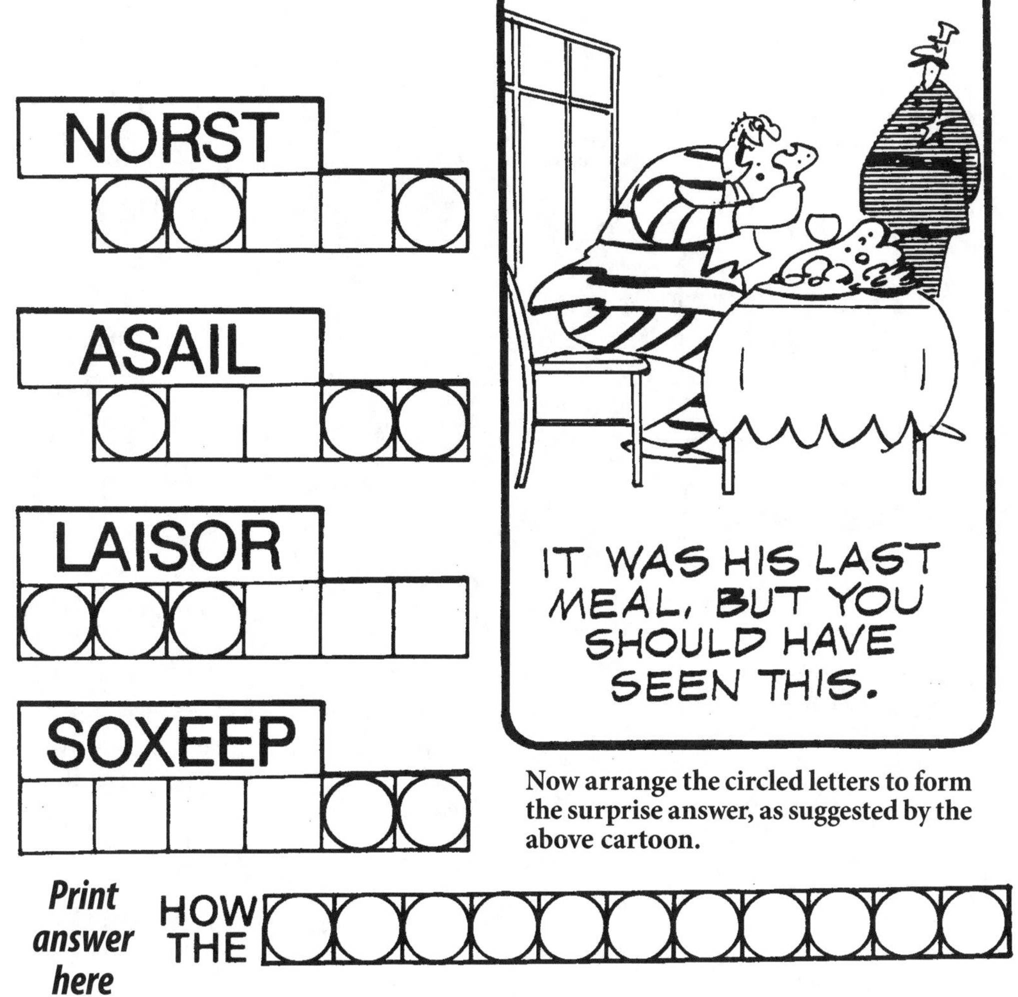
NORST
ASAIL
LAISOR
SOXEEP
IT WAS HIS LAST MEAL, BUT YOU SHOULD HAVE SEEN THIS.

Now arrange the circled letters to form the surprise answer, as suggested by the above cartoon.

Print answer here HOW THE

PUZZLE
21

JUMBLE®

Unscramble these four Jumbles, one letter to each square, to form four ordinary words.

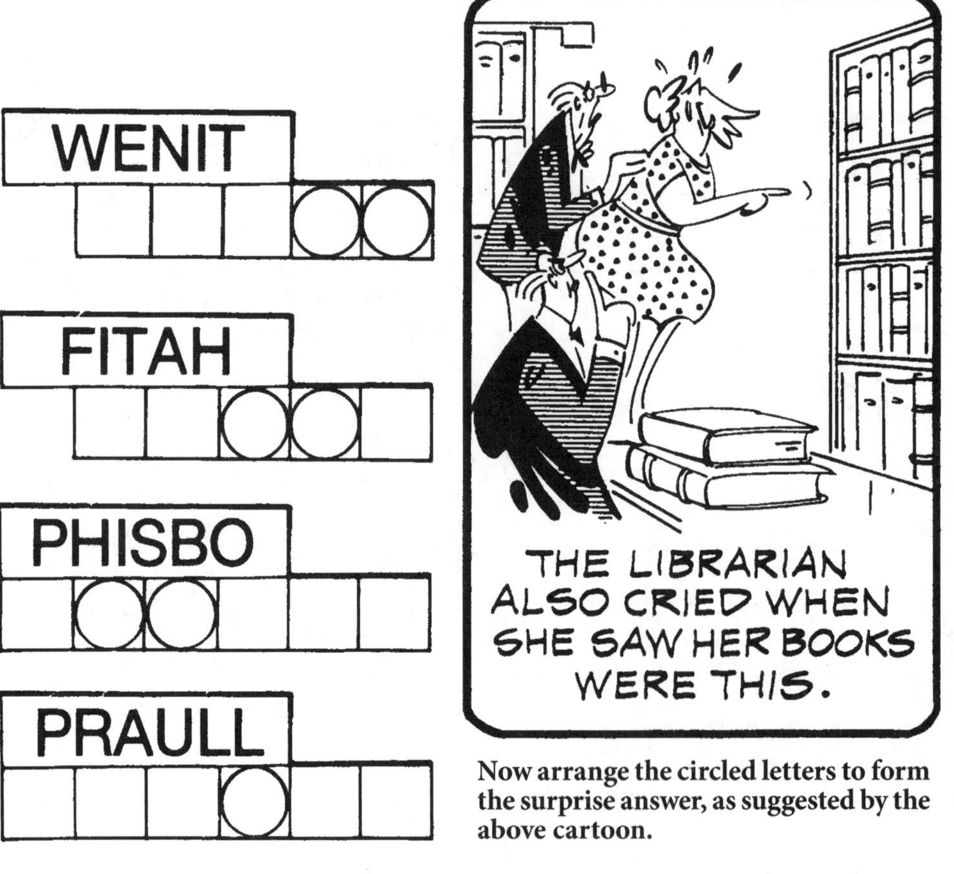
WENIT
FITAH
PHISBO
PRAULL
THE LIBRARIAN ALSO CRIED WHEN SHE SAW HER BOOKS WERE THIS.

Now arrange the circled letters to form the surprise answer, as suggested by the above cartoon.

Print answer here ◯◯ "◯◯◯◯◯"

PUZZLE
22

JUMBLE®

Unscramble these four Jumbles, one letter to each square, to form four ordinary words.

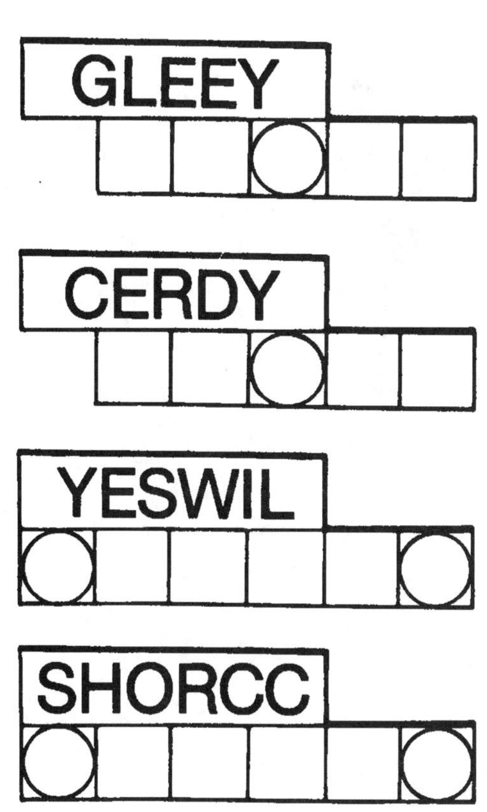
GLEEY
CERDY
YESWIL
SHORCC

But he won't eat any pet food I buy him!
WHAT THAT FINICKY DOG WAS.

Now arrange the circled letters to form the surprise answer, as suggested by the above cartoon.

Print answer here " ◯◯◯◯-◯◯ "

PUZZLE
23

JUMBLE®

Unscramble these four Jumbles, one letter to each square, to form four ordinary words.

BICUT

WHASA

TALLYF

CENTED

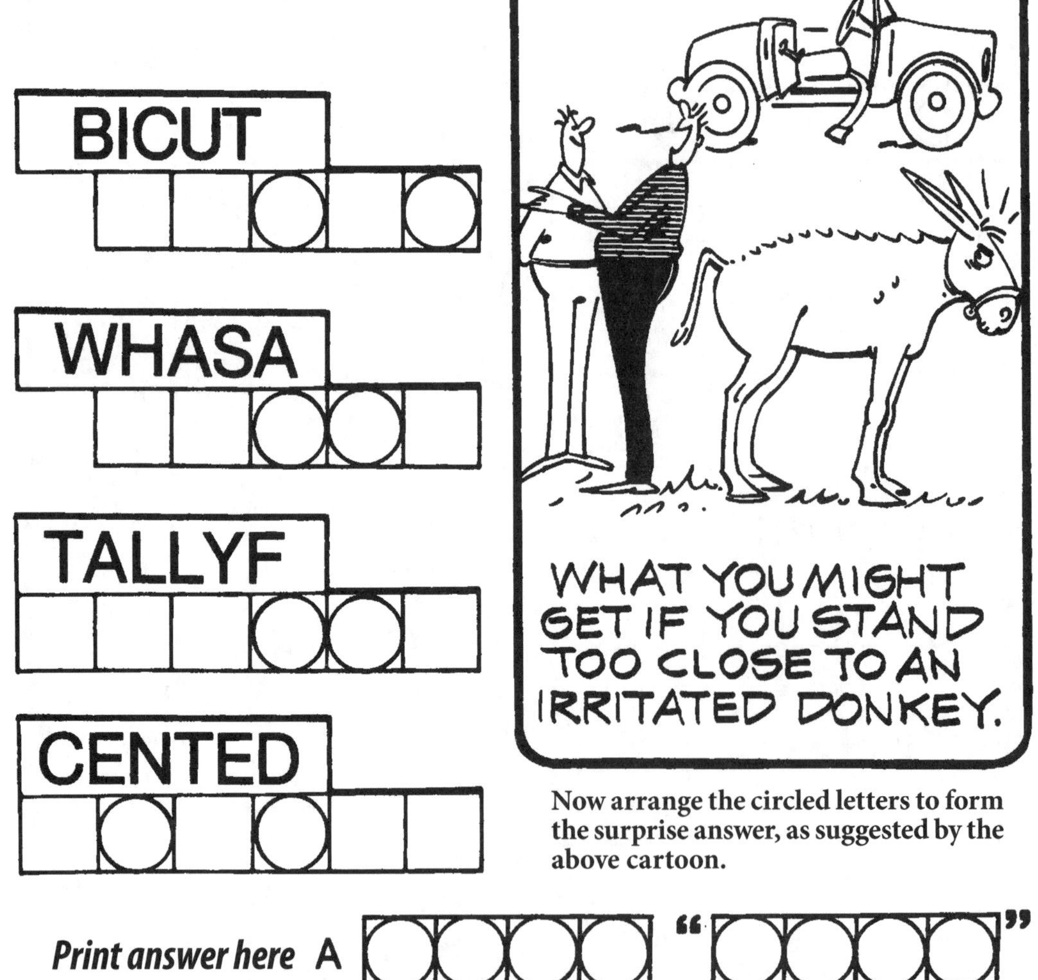
WHAT YOU MIGHT GET IF YOU STAND TOO CLOSE TO AN IRRITATED DONKEY.

Now arrange the circled letters to form the surprise answer, as suggested by the above cartoon.

Print answer here A ◯◯◯◯ "◯◯◯◯"

PUZZLE
24

JUMBLE®

Unscramble these four Jumbles, one letter to each square, to form four ordinary words.

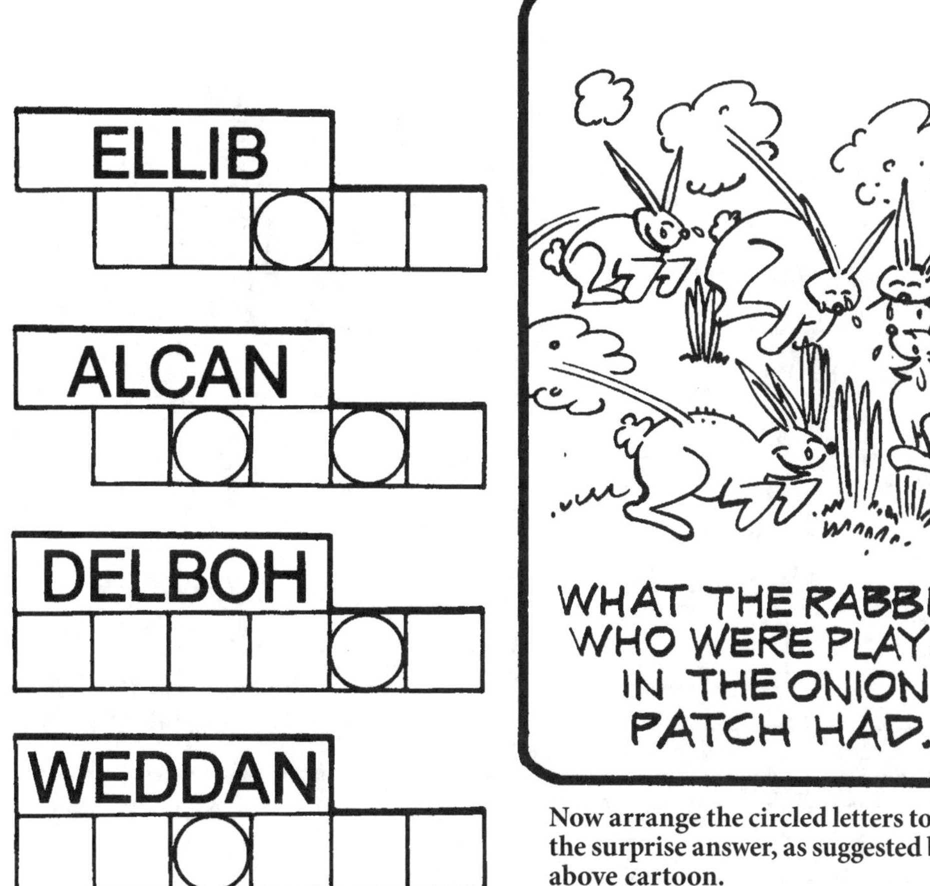
ELLIB
ALCAN
DELBOH
WEDDAN
WHAT THE RABBITS WHO WERE PLAYING IN THE ONION PATCH HAD.

Now arrange the circled letters to form the surprise answer, as suggested by the above cartoon.

Print answer here ◯ “◯◯◯◯”

PUZZLE
25

JUMBLE®

Unscramble these four Jumbles, one letter to each square, to form four ordinary words.

NEFIT

TCHAB

GANDEA

WABILE

HE WAS ALWAYS GOING AROUND IN CIRCLES BECAUSE HE THOUGHT HE WAS THIS.

Now arrange the circled letters to form the surprise answer, as suggested by the above cartoon.

Print answer here A

JUMBLE®
Parachute

Daily
Puzzles

PUZZLE
26

JUMBLE®

Unscramble these four Jumbles, one letter to each square, to form four ordinary words.

POTIV

ROHON

IMUSSE

KINIBI

But. . .
but. . .
BILL
BILL
WHAT THE GAMBLING ADDICT HAD TROUBLE BALANCING.

Now arrange the circled letters to form the surprise answer, as suggested by the above cartoon.

Print answer here

PUZZLE
27

JUMBLE®

Unscramble these four Jumbles, one letter to each square, to form four ordinary words.

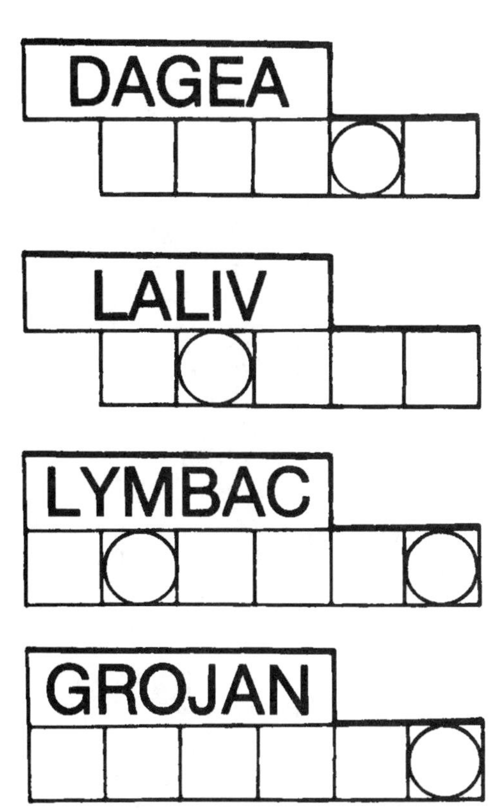
DAGEA
LALIV
LYMBAC
GROJAN

Hey, Boss—you should have been a pro
A HYPOCRITE IS SOMEONE WHO CAN'T TELL THE TRUTH WITH-OUT DOING THIS.

Now arrange the circled letters to form the surprise answer, as suggested by the above cartoon.

Print answer here 

PUZZLE
28

JUMBLE®

Unscramble these four Jumbles, one letter to each square, to form four ordinary words.

CHEKT

STAIV

YETLEE

SUNGUF

CAN YOU GET FUR FROM A SKUNK?

Now arrange the circled letters to form the surprise answer, as suggested by the above cartoon.

Print answer here " ◯◯ YOU'RE ◯◯◯◯◯ "

PUZZLE
29

JUMBLE®

Unscramble these four Jumbles, one letter to each square, to form four ordinary words.

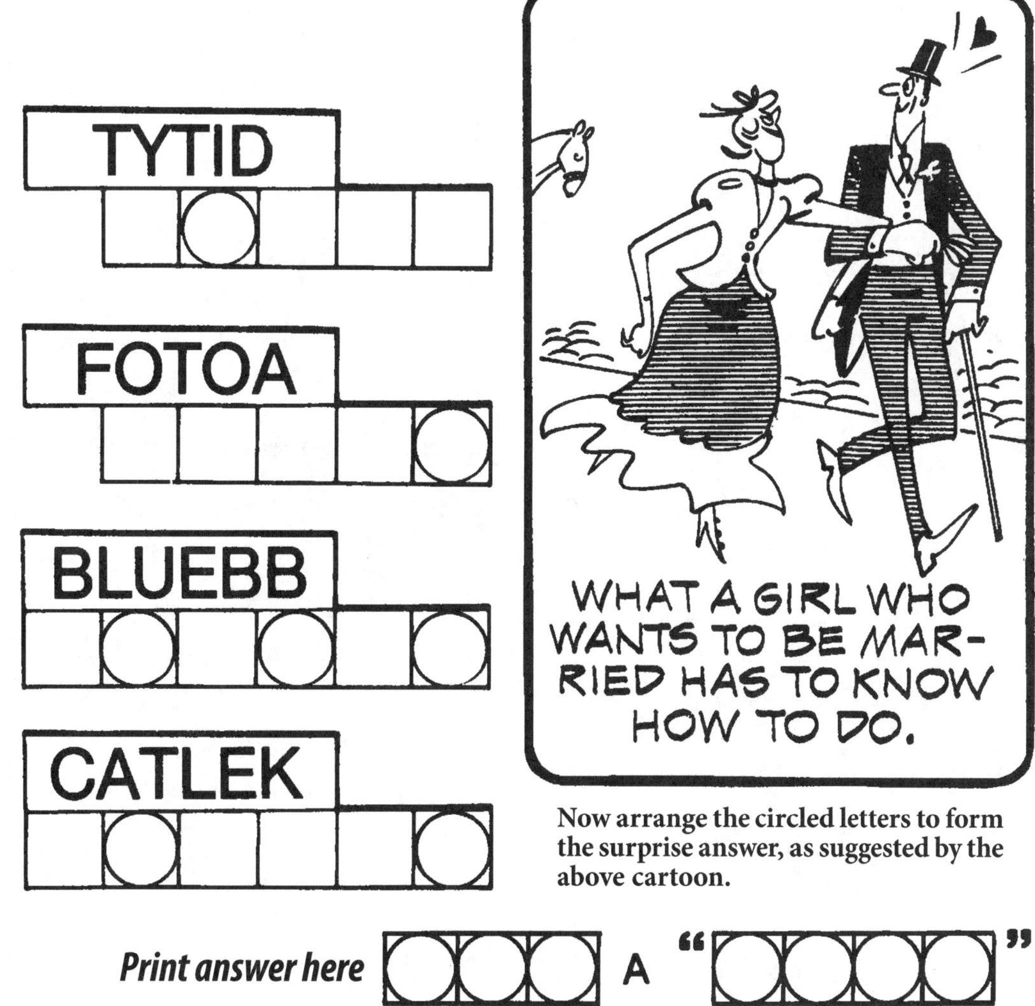
TYTID
FOTOA
BLUEBB
CATLEK
WHAT A GIRL WHO WANTS TO BE MAR-RIED HAS TO KNOW HOW TO DO.
Now arrange the circled letters to form the surprise answer, as suggested by the above cartoon.
Print answer here
A “ ”

PUZZLE
30

JUMBLE®

Unscramble these four Jumbles, one letter to each square, to form four ordinary words.

DYLAL
FITEB
CORRET
HUMILE
How about a movie?
OBITS
WHAT SHE CALLED THAT SOUR HUSBAND OF HERS.

Now arrange the circled letters to form the surprise answer, as suggested by the above cartoon.

Print answer here HER "◯◯◯◯◯◯" ◯◯◯◯

PUZZLE
31

JUMBLE®

Unscramble these four Jumbles, one letter to each square, to form four ordinary words.

GEMID
BOMUG
ZURBEZ
LAMORN

WHAT THE COACH DID EVERY TIME A PLAYER FUMBLED.

Now arrange the circled letters to form the surprise answer, as suggested by the above cartoon.

Print answer here

PUZZLE
32

JUMBLE®

Unscramble these four Jumbles, one letter to each square, to form four ordinary words.

HAWSS
SURBT
EVILAB
CLUPEO
WHAT A BEAUTY CONTEST JUDGE HAS TO KNOW HOW TO DO.

Now arrange the circled letters to form the surprise answer, as suggested by the above cartoon.

Print answer here ON

PUZZLE
33

JUMBLE®

Unscramble these four Jumbles, one letter to each square, to form four ordinary words.

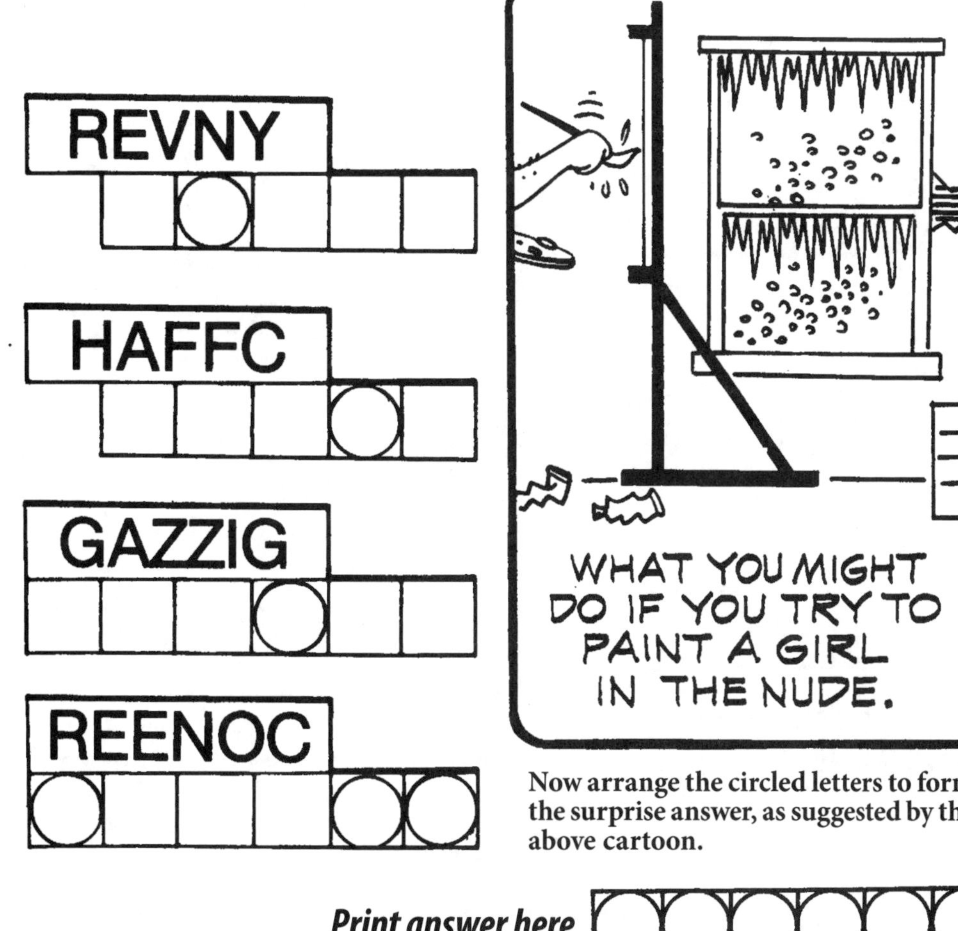
REVNY
HAFFC
GAZZIG
REENOC
WHAT YOU MIGHT DO IF YOU TRY TO PAINT A GIRL IN THE NUDE.

Now arrange the circled letters to form the surprise answer, as suggested by the above cartoon.

Print answer here

PUZZLE
34

JUMBLE®

Unscramble these four Jumbles, one letter to each square, to form four ordinary words.

RUHYR

SINEA

NINTTE

INDOOM

What's the matter—nothing good enough for you?
SHE COULDN'T COOK WORTH A DARN, BUT SHE SURE KNEW HOW TO DO THIS.

Now arrange the circled letters to form the surprise answer, as suggested by the above cartoon.

Print answer here

PUZZLE
35

JUMBLE®

Unscramble these four Jumbles, one letter to each square, to form four ordinary words.

MUTAG
ORXYP
SINOUF
BOTERD
THEY DECIDED TO APPOINT HIM CHIEF COOK BECAUSE HE HAD THIS.

Now arrange the circled letters to form the surprise answer, as suggested by the above cartoon.

Print answer here THE "◯◯◯" ◯◯◯◯ ◯◯

PUZZLE
36

JUMBLE®

Unscramble these four Jumbles, one letter to each square, to form four ordinary words.

HAKSY
TABLO
UNTEAR
DIPEEM
Sleeping again!
SAMSON LOVED DELILAH UNTIL SHE DID THIS.
Print answer here
“ ”

Now arrange the circled letters to form the surprise answer, as suggested by the above cartoon.

PUZZLE
37

JUMBLE®

Unscramble these four Jumbles, one letter to each square, to form four ordinary words.

LAVIT
CUMSI
TIENNY
CLIFEK
WHY HE INSISTED ON WEARING SEAT BELTS.

Now arrange the circled letters to form the surprise answer, as suggested by the above cartoon.

Print answer here TO ◯◯◯◯ HIS ◯◯◯

PUZZLE
38

JUMBLE®

Unscramble these four Jumbles, one letter to each square, to form four ordinary words.

RUPOC

VARAL

RAWHOR

BOLGEN

HOW MANY POUNDS OF LIMBURGER CHEESE DO YOU WANT?

Now arrange the circled letters to form the surprise answer, as suggested by the above cartoon.

Print answer here " "

PUZZLE
39

JUMBLE®

Unscramble these four Jumbles, one letter to each square, to form four ordinary words.

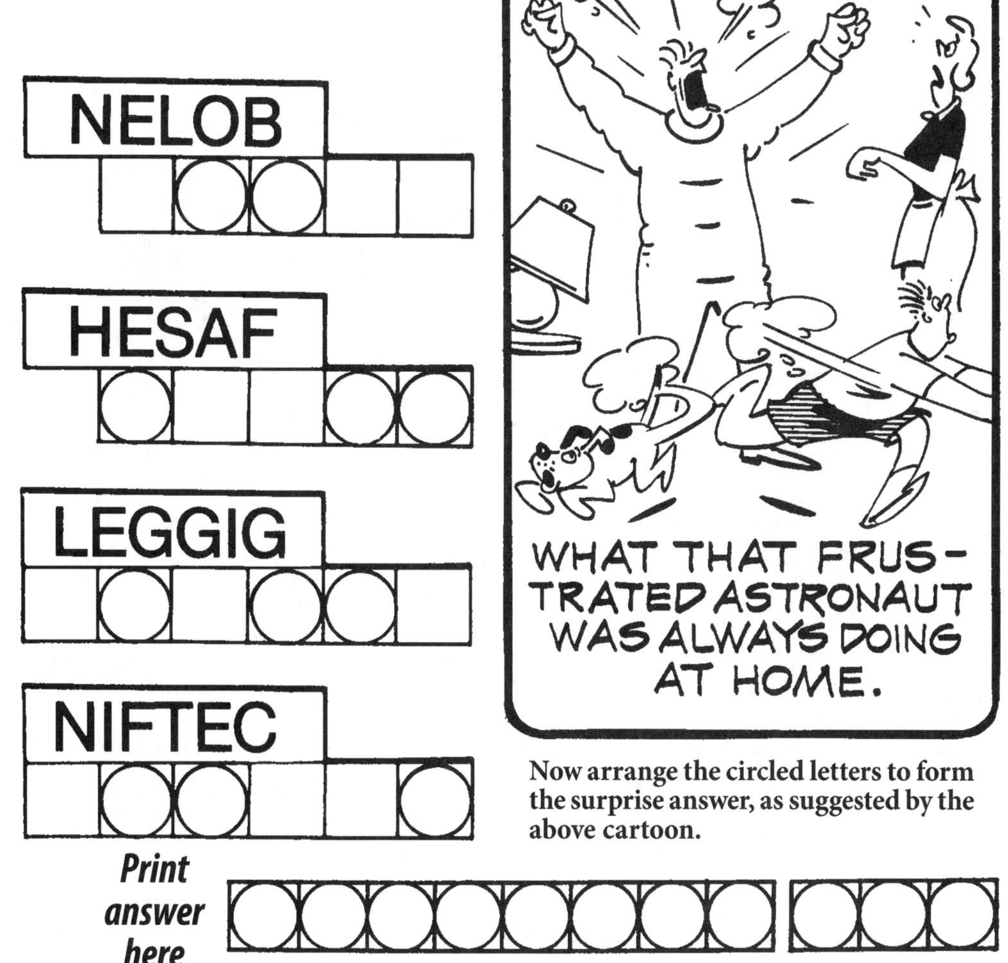
NELOB
HESAF
LEGGIG
NIFTEC
WHAT THAT FRUS-TRATED ASTRONAUT WAS ALWAYS DOING AT HOME.
Now arrange the circled letters to form the surprise answer, as suggested by the above cartoon.
Print answer here

PUZZLE
40

JUMBLE®

Unscramble these four Jumbles, one letter to each square, to form four ordinary words.

STACE

NARBD

GETURT

BUCTAD

It sure took nerve to get where he got
ALTHOUGH MAN DOES NOT LIVE BY BREAD ALONE, HE MAY GET BY ON THIS.

Now arrange the circled letters to form the surprise answer, as suggested by the above cartoon.

Print answer here " "

PUZZLE
41

JUMBLE®

Unscramble these four Jumbles, one letter to each square, to form four ordinary words.

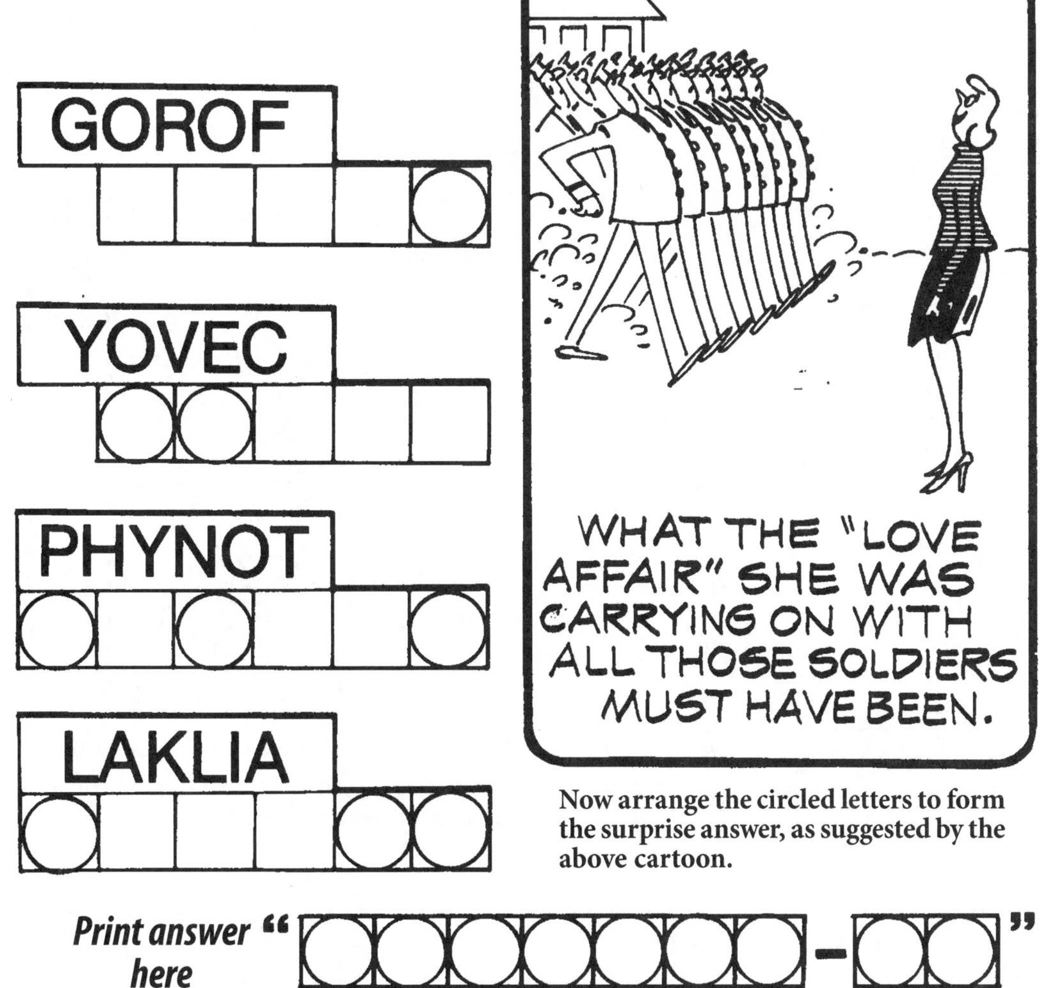
GOROF
YOVEC
PHYNOT
LAKLIA
WHAT THE "LOVE AFFAIR" SHE WAS CARRYING ON WITH ALL THOSE SOLDIERS MUST HAVE BEEN.

Now arrange the circled letters to form the surprise answer, as suggested by the above cartoon.

Print answer here "◯◯◯◯◯◯◯-◯◯"

PUZZLE
42

JUMBLE®

Unscramble these four Jumbles, one letter to each square, to form four ordinary words.

ULARR
LABAN
WUNSIE
PORTIM
A FEELING YOU GET WHEN YOU OPEN YOUR MAIL ON THE FIRST OF THE MONTH.

Now arrange the circled letters to form the surprise answer, as suggested by the above cartoon.

Print answer here "◯◯◯◯-◯◯◯◯"

PUZZLE
43

JUMBLE®

Unscramble these four Jumbles, one letter to each square, to form four ordinary words.

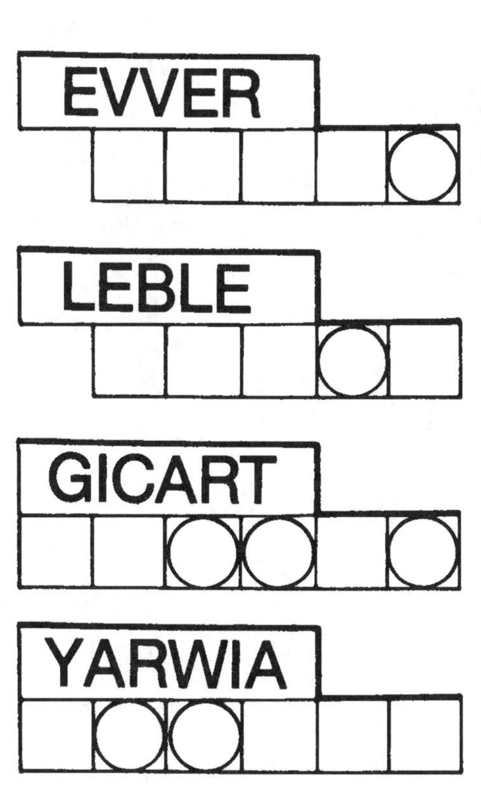
EVVER
LEBLE
GICART
YARWIA

WHAT THEY CALLED THE MAN WHO PUT GLASS INTO THE IGLOO WINDOWS.

Now arrange the circled letters to form the surprise answer, as suggested by the above cartoon.

Print answer here THE "  "

PUZZLE
44

JUMBLE®

Unscramble these four Jumbles, one letter to each square, to form four ordinary words.

GALEE

SYSAG

TINEKT

STYMIC

WHAT THAT LONG TOUR MADE HIM.

Now arrange the circled letters to form the surprise answer, as suggested by the above cartoon.

Print answer here " ◯◯◯ " ◯◯◯◯

PUZZLE
45

JUMBLE®

Unscramble these four Jumbles, one letter to each square, to form four ordinary words.

ORVAS
TWAHR
WOFELL
TEXMEP
WHAT HIS NEIGHBOR SAID WHEN HE SHOWED OFF HIS NEW LAWN EQUIPMENT.

Now arrange the circled letters to form the surprise answer, as suggested by the above cartoon.

Print answer here "◯◯◯◯◯◯" ◯◯◯◯◯◯ TO YOU

PUZZLE
46

JUMBLE®

Unscramble these four Jumbles, one letter to each square, to form four ordinary words.

OXTIN
SINUM
HARANG
INGRIF
YE OLDE
WHAT THOSE BOXERS ENGAGED IN WHILE HAVING A FEW DRINKS.

Now arrange the circled letters to form the surprise answer, as suggested by the above cartoon.

Print answer here " "

PUZZLE
47

JUMBLE®

Unscramble these four Jumbles, one letter to each square, to form four ordinary words.

BODUT
YAMOF
VEEVOL
MUDINS
JEWELRY
WHEN SHE ASKED FOR A DIAMOND, HE TURNED THIS.

Now arrange the circled letters to form the surprise answer, as suggested by the above cartoon.

Print answer here " "

JUMBLE®

Unscramble these four Jumbles, one letter to each square, to form four ordinary words.

LORBI

HARAJ

KELLIY

SPATOL

ORTHOPEDIC SURGEONS MUST BE LUCKY WHEN THEY GET THIS.

Now arrange the circled letters to form the surprise answer, as suggested by the above cartoon.

Print answer here ○○○ THE "○○○○○○○"

PUZZLE
49

JUMBLE®

Unscramble these four Jumbles, one letter to each square, to form four ordinary words.

PYLAP

HARCI

TRIVED

NUHRGY

WHAT KIND OF YOUNGSTER DOES BASKETBALL USUALLY ATTRACT?

Now arrange the circled letters to form the surprise answer, as suggested by the above cartoon.

Print answer here A VERY

PUZZLE
50

JUMBLE®

Unscramble these four Jumbles, one letter to each square, to form four ordinary words.

RYFIA

TELIE

REDOWP

CLAUHN

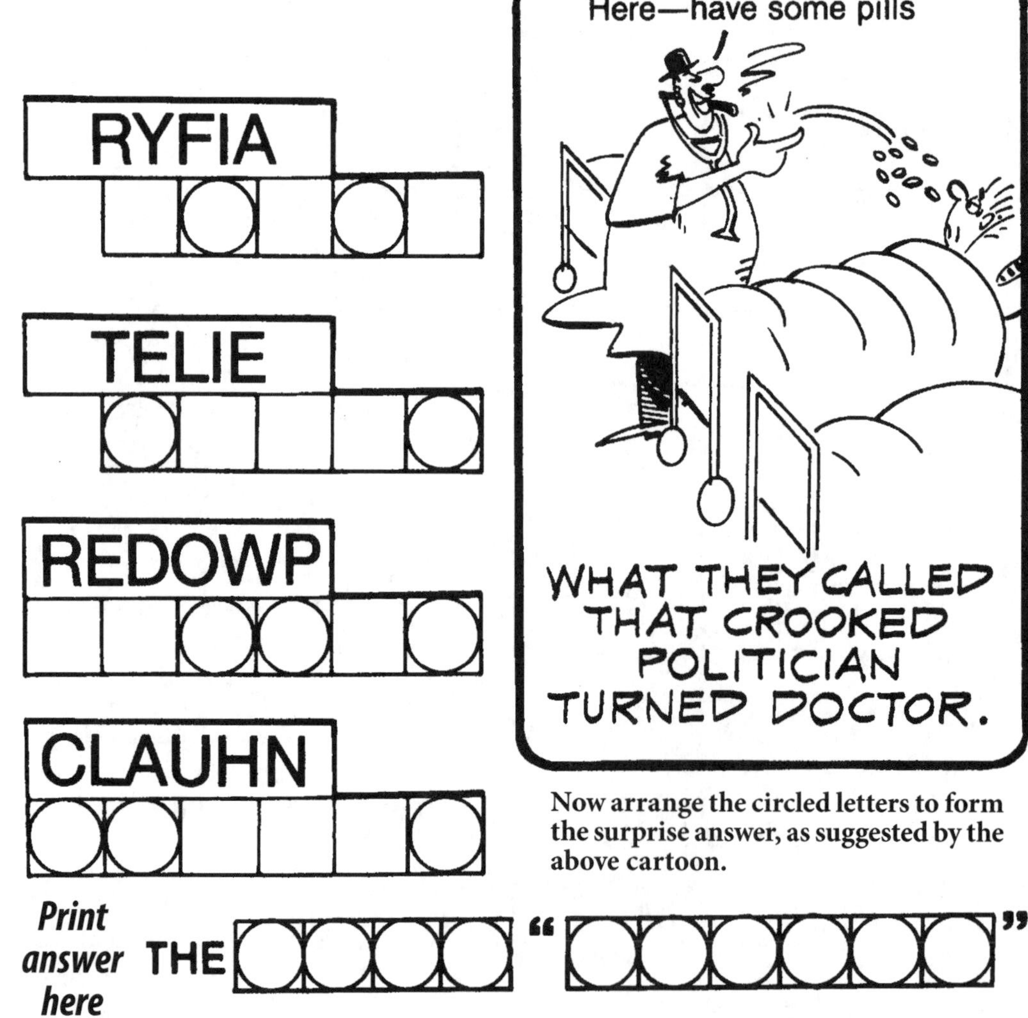
Here—have some pills
WHAT THEY CALLED THAT CROOKED POLITICIAN TURNED DOCTOR.

Now arrange the circled letters to form the surprise answer, as suggested by the above cartoon.

Print answer here THE “ ”

PUZZLE
51

JUMBLE®

Unscramble these four Jumbles, one letter to each square, to form four ordinary words.

TIDOT
WETHA
RYCKIT
WHALLO
10-31
HOW CHILDREN ARRIVE AT YOUR DOOR TONIGHT.

Now arrange the circled letters to form the surprise answer, as suggested by the above cartoon.

Print answer here EVERY "◯◯◯◯◯" ◯◯◯

PUZZLE
52

JUMBLE®

Unscramble these four Jumbles, one letter to each square, to form four ordinary words.

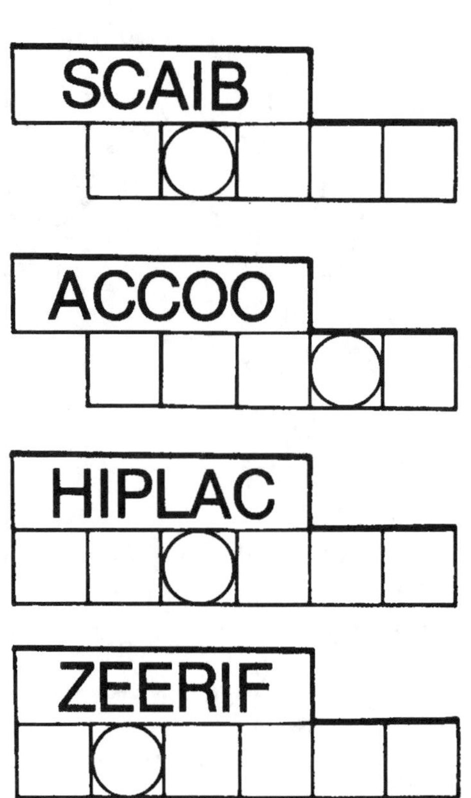
SCAIB
ACCOO
HIPLAC
ZEERIF

Always makes me nervous
IT'S "SAID" TO BE A TEST.

Now arrange the circled letters to form the surprise answer, as suggested by the above cartoon.

Print answer here “  ”

PUZZLE
53

JUMBLE®

Unscramble these four Jumbles, one letter to each square, to form four ordinary words.

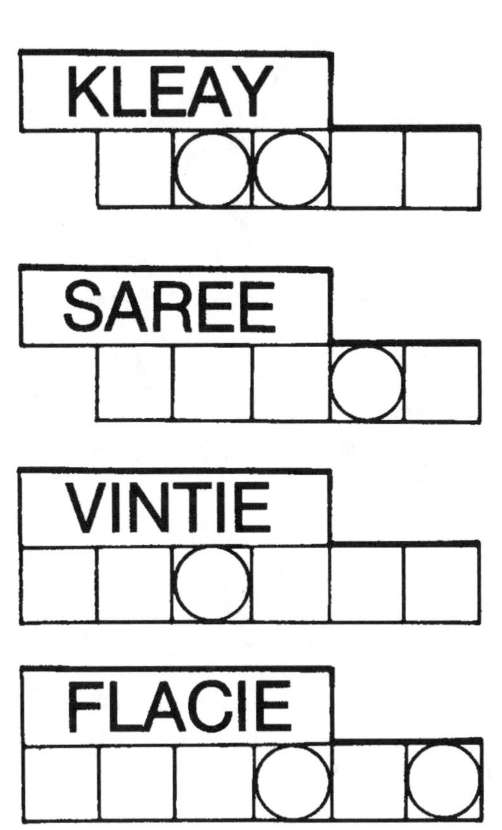
KLEAY
SAREE
VINTIE
FLACIE

He believes everything he hears
But it's in one ear and out the other
WHAT TOO MUCH OF AN OPEN MIND MIGHT BE LIKE.

Now arrange the circled letters to form the surprise answer, as suggested by the above cartoon.

Print answer here 

PUZZLE
54

JUMBLE®

Unscramble these four Jumbles, one letter to each square, to form four ordinary words.

PERPI
LEEXI
KAUMPE
PREMAT
ANOTHER NAME FOR A PAWNBROKER.

Now arrange the circled letters to form the surprise answer, as suggested by the above cartoon.

Print answer here A "   "

PUZZLE
55

JUMBLE®

Unscramble these four Jumbles, one letter to each square, to form four ordinary words.

TRUPE

ROFOL

LEUXED

GREESY

AT THE SEASHORE, YOUR COMPOSURE IS OFTEN DISTRACTED BY THIS.

Now arrange the circled letters to form the surprise answer, as suggested by the above cartoon.

Print answer here

PUZZLE
56

JUMBLE®

Unscramble these four Jumbles, one letter to each square, to form four ordinary words.

THAPC

VILIC

UPCHIC

GAUHTT

WHAT A MARRIAGE PROPOSAL IS.

Now arrange the circled letters to form the surprise answer, as suggested by the above cartoon.

Print answer here A

PUZZLE
57

JUMBLE®

Unscramble these four Jumbles, one letter to each square, to form four ordinary words.

EMZIA
GINOG
ODUXTE
INCLEP
THE ONLY REASON THEY CALLED HIM A BIG SHOT WAS THAT HE WAS ALWAYS DOING THIS.

Now arrange the circled letters to form the surprise answer, as suggested by the above cartoon.

Print answer here

PUZZLE
58

JUMBLE®

Unscramble these four Jumbles, one letter to each square, to form four ordinary words.

DOBOL

KOPER

NUTHAG

GUMSED

WHAT THAT GOOD-LOOKING DOG WAS.

Now arrange the circled letters to form the surprise answer, as suggested by the above cartoon.

Print answer here " "

PUZZLE
59

JUMBLE®

Unscramble these four Jumbles, one letter to each square, to form four ordinary words.

TILOP
GACIM
RECUPS
CUNESS
He's always insulting people!
YOU'D GET NO PRAISES FROM THIS.

Now arrange the circled letters to form the surprise answer, as suggested by the above cartoon.

Print answer here AN " "

PUZZLE
60

JUMBLE®

Unscramble these four Jumbles, one letter to each square, to form four ordinary words.

NERTY
MILPE
HACTLE
SMABAL
WHERE ARMAMENTS MIGHT BE FOUND, NATURALLY.
Now arrange the circled letters to form the surprise answer, as suggested by the above cartoon.
Print answer here
AMONG "___-__-_____"

PUZZLE
61

JUMBLE®

Unscramble these four Jumbles, one letter to each square, to form four ordinary words.

BORNI
MILTI
TRIMAN
UNBOAD
He should be mowing the lawn
WHAT SHE CALLED HER HUSBAND WHO WAS AN AMATEUR ORNITHOLOGIST.

Now arrange the circled letters to form the surprise answer, as suggested by the above cartoon.

Print answer here " "

PUZZLE
62

JUMBLE®

Unscramble these four Jumbles, one letter to each square, to form four ordinary words.

BOANT
LAGIE
JENNIO
RITHEH

She's never had to worry about money
WHAT TO DO IN ORDER TO HAVE SOFT WHITE HANDS.

Now arrange the circled letters to form the surprise answer, as suggested by the above cartoon.

Print answer here

PUZZLE
63

JUMBLE®

Unscramble these four Jumbles, one letter to each square, to form four ordinary words.

DEVEL
VEENT
PAPNYS
SIFOSY
ON THE AIR
WHAT THE NERVOUS DISC JOCKEY LIVES ON.

Now arrange the circled letters to form the surprise answer, as suggested by the above cartoon.

Print answer here &

PUZZLE
64

JUMBLE®

Unscramble these four Jumbles, one letter to each square, to form four ordinary words.

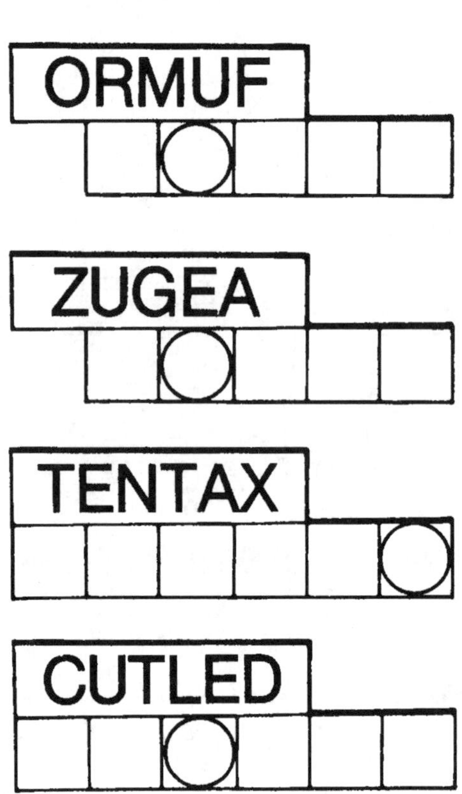
ORMUF
ZUGEA
TENTAX
CUTLED

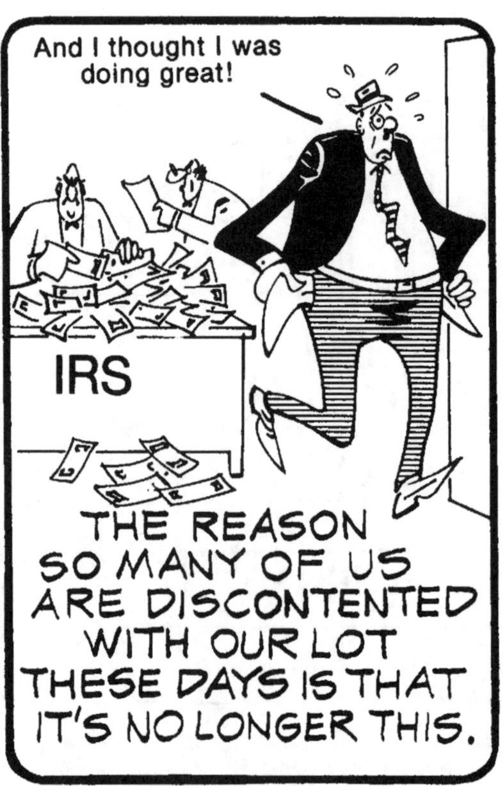
And I thought I was doing great!
IRS
THE REASON SO MANY OF US ARE DISCONTENTED WITH OUR LOT THESE DAYS IS THAT IT'S NO LONGER THIS.

Now arrange the circled letters to form the surprise answer, as suggested by the above cartoon.

Print answer here 

PUZZLE
65

JUMBLE®

Unscramble these four Jumbles, one letter to each square, to form four ordinary words.

YEEND

PREYK

SLIMIE

INTOAR

STEAKS and CHOPS
WHAT LIFE WAS FOR THE GUY WHO SPENT ALL HIS TIME AT THAT "SINGLES" SPOT.

Now arrange the circled letters to form the surprise answer, as suggested by the above cartoon.

Print answer here JUST "◯◯◯◯" & ◯◯◯◯◯

PUZZLE
66

JUMBLE®

Unscramble these four Jumbles, one letter to each square, to form four ordinary words.

MUTOH

PARAT

GANDIL

THRENE

WHAT A WOMAN MIGHT ATTEMPT TO DRAW WITH AN EYEBROW PENCIL.

Now arrange the circled letters to form the surprise answer, as suggested by the above cartoon.

Print answer here

PUZZLE
67

JUMBLE®

Unscramble these four Jumbles, one letter to each square, to form four ordinary words.

YOSIN
LYDIO
TRYSAP
MUDINS
He'll never get anywhere acting like that
THIS MAY DETERMINE WHAT KIND OF POSITION YOU HAVE IN LIFE.

Now arrange the circled letters to form the surprise answer, as suggested by the above cartoon.

Print answer here YOUR

PUZZLE
68

JUMBLE®

Unscramble these four Jumbles, one letter to each square, to form four ordinary words.

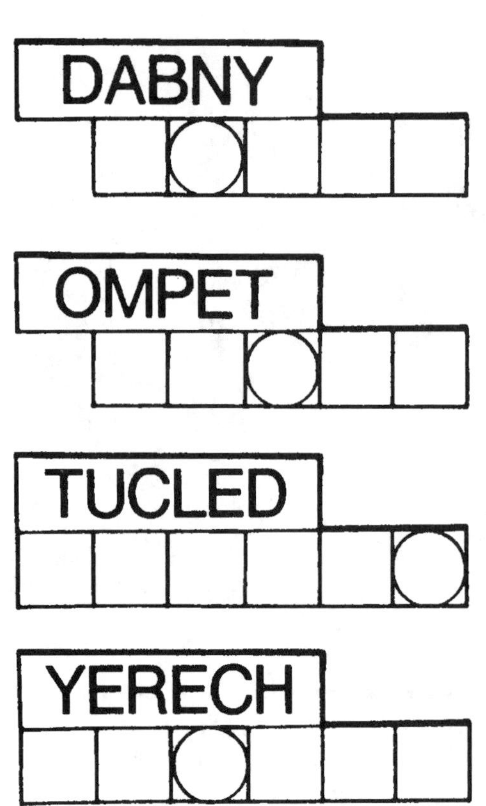
DABNY
OMPET
TUCLED
YERECH

Wait'll I get finished with him!
WHAT THE "HAM" WAS FOR THE DRAMA CRITIC.

Now arrange the circled letters to form the surprise answer, as suggested by the above cartoon.

Print answer here HIS "◯◯◯◯"

PUZZLE
69

JUMBLE®

Unscramble these four Jumbles, one letter to each square, to form four ordinary words.

INEEC
PRUCO
PEEXOS
SAHVNI
Lovely! I'll take three of them!
$
HE CALLED HER "DEAR" BEFORE MARRIAGE AND AFTERWARDS THIS.

Now arrange the circled letters to form the surprise answer, as suggested by the above cartoon.

Print answer here " "

PUZZLE
70

JUMBLE®

Unscramble these four Jumbles, one letter to each square, to form four ordinary words.

NOPLY
DUGEF
CHAWES
TRIEHD
Get lost!
A GIRL WHO NOW TELLS HIM WHERE TO TAKE HER MIGHT LATER TELL HIM THIS.
Now arrange the circled letters to form the surprise answer, as suggested by the above cartoon.
Print answer here
TO

PUZZLE
71

JUMBLE®

Unscramble these four Jumbles, one letter to each square, to form four ordinary words.

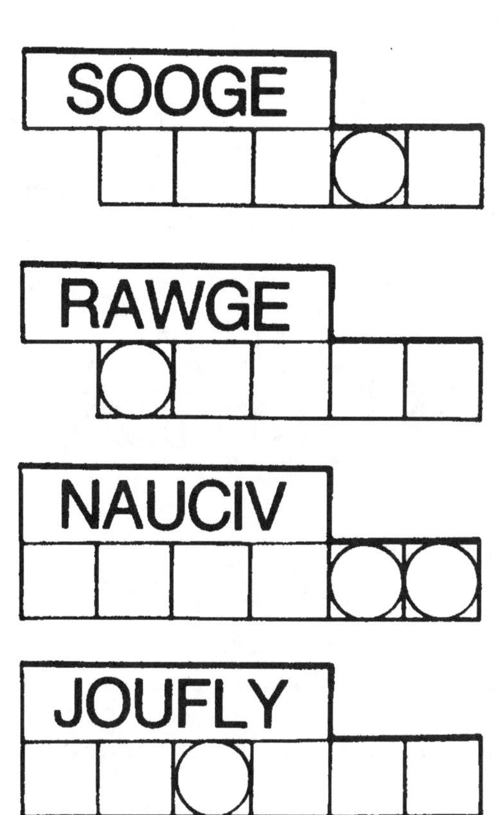
SOOGE
RAWGE
NAUCIV
JOUFLY

THAT BIG TALKER'S LISTENERS GOT NO CHANCE TO OPEN THEIR MOUTHS EXCEPT FOR THIS.

Now arrange the circled letters to form the surprise answer, as suggested by the above cartoon.

Print answer here 

PUZZLE
72

JUMBLE®

Unscramble these four Jumbles, one letter to each square, to form four ordinary words.

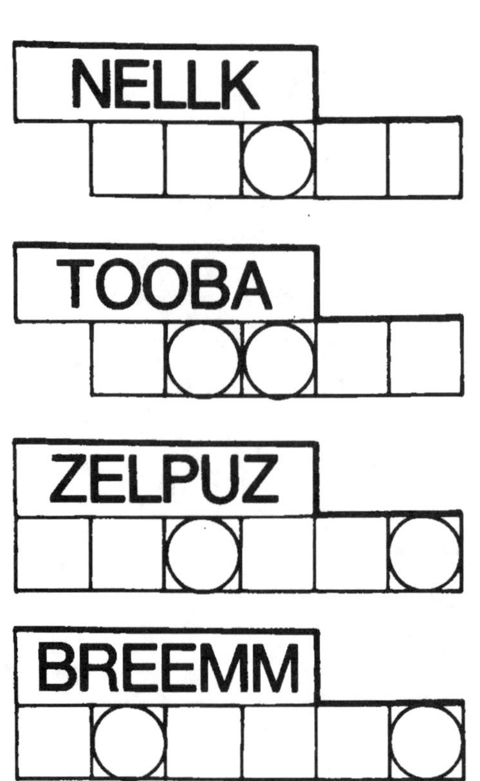
NELLK
TOOBA
ZELPUZ
BREEMM

It's sure riding easy
WHAT SAILING A BOAT ON A NICE WINDY DAY CAN BE.

Now arrange the circled letters to form the surprise answer, as suggested by the above cartoon.

Print answer here

PUZZLE
73

JUMBLE®

Unscramble these four Jumbles, one letter to each square, to form four ordinary words.

SVORI
IDDEC
DAYPOR
SPEBIC
I've had it with you
WHAT SHE DID WHEN SHE DIS-COVERED THAT HER BOYFRIEND WAS A CROOKED GAMBLER.

Now arrange the circled letters to form the surprise answer, as suggested by the above cartoon.

Print answer here "☐☐☐-☐☐☐☐☐☐" HIM

PUZZLE
74

JUMBLE®

Unscramble these four Jumbles, one letter to each square, to form four ordinary words.

TEELI

KEROP

YABSUW

LENKER

He's always robbing other people's ideas
ANOTHER NAME FOR A PLAGIARIST.

Now arrange the circled letters to form the surprise answer, as suggested by the above cartoon.

Print answer here A " "

PUZZLE
75

JUMBLE®

Unscramble these four Jumbles, one letter to each square, to form four ordinary words.

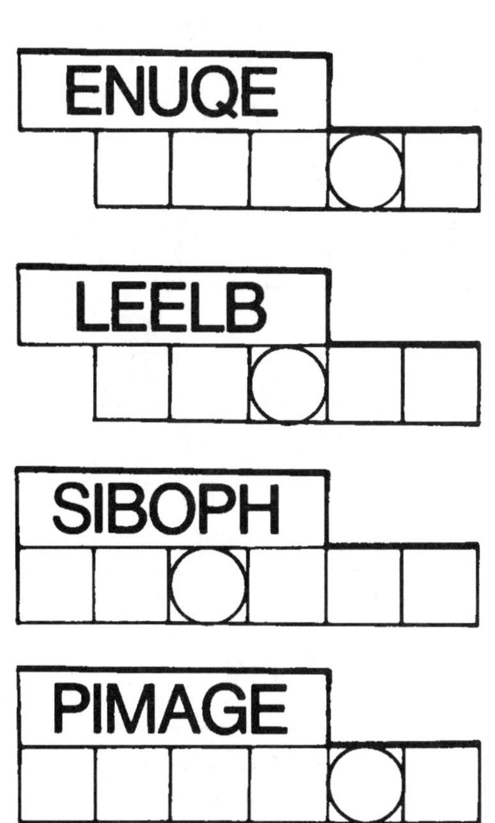
ENUQE
LEELB
SIBOPH
PIMAGE

A FISHERMAN SOME-TIMES STANDS STILL WHILE FISHING, BUT MORE OFTEN DOES THIS.

Now arrange the circled letters to form the surprise answer, as suggested by the above cartoon.

Print answer here

PUZZLE
76

JUMBLE®

Unscramble these four Jumbles, one letter to each square, to form four ordinary words.

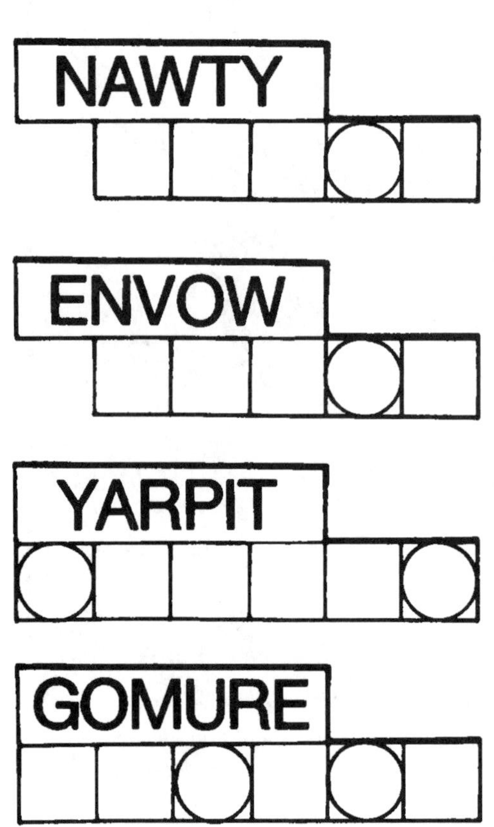
NAWTY
ENVOW
YARPIT
GOMURE

Another rejection!
Why don't you go out and get a construction job?
WHAT AN UNTALENTED WRITER MIGHT EARN BY HIS PEN.

Now arrange the circled letters to form the surprise answer, as suggested by the above cartoon.

Print answer here 

PUZZLE
77

JUMBLE®

Unscramble these four Jumbles, one letter to each square, to form four ordinary words.

SIVAT
LANTA
CHOSOL
REBAYT
What did I ever see in that one?
?
!
WHAT HER OLD FLAME TURNED OUT TO BE.
A “ ”

Now arrange the circled letters to form the surprise answer, as suggested by the above cartoon.

Print answer here

PUZZLE
78

JUMBLE®

Unscramble these four Jumbles, one letter to each square, to form four ordinary words.

IXAMM

UPTYT

BOWELL

CRALIG

I can only give you a little clue, maybe more tomorrow
HOW THE SCANDAL-MONGER LET THE CAT OUT OF THE BAG.

Now arrange the circled letters to form the surprise answer, as suggested by the above cartoon.

Print answer here ONE ◯◯◯◯◯ AT A ◯◯◯◯◯

PUZZLE
79

JUMBLE®

Unscramble these four Jumbles, one letter to each square, to form four ordinary words.

TOIDT
LAASI
CHALUN
UPLARB
WHAT KIND OF JOKES DO THOSE MOUNTAIN FOLK TELL?
Print answer here
" - " ONES

Now arrange the circled letters to form the surprise answer, as suggested by the above cartoon.

PUZZLE
80

JUMBLE®

Unscramble these four Jumbles, one letter to each square, to form four ordinary words.

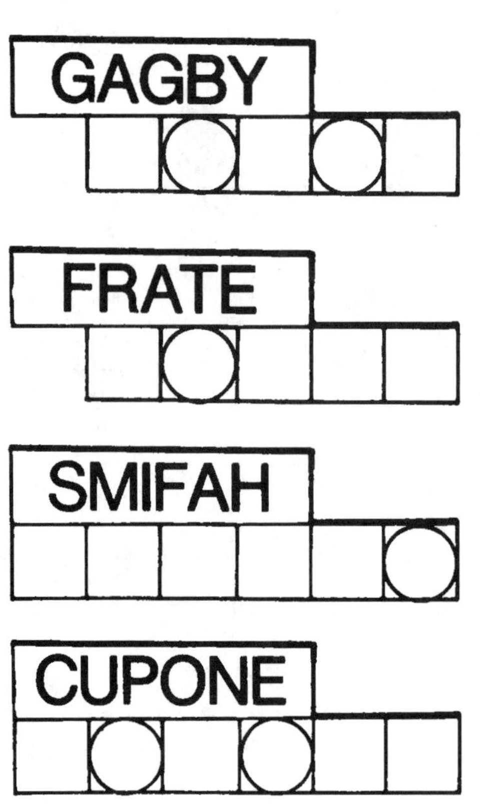
GAGBY
FRATE
SMIFAH
CUPONE

WALLPAPERING IS EASY ONCE YOU GET THIS.

Now arrange the circled letters to form the surprise answer, as suggested by the above cartoon.

Print answer here THE   IT

PUZZLE
81

JUMBLE®

Unscramble these four Jumbles, one letter to each square, to form four ordinary words.

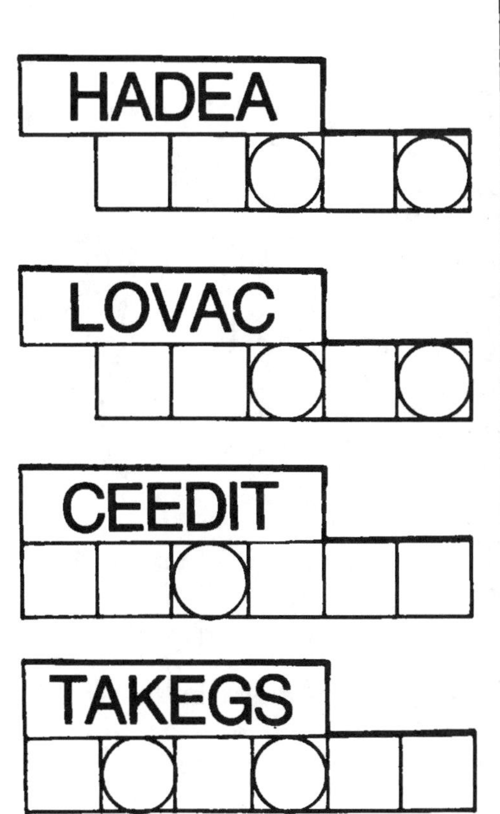
HADEA
LOVAC
CEEDIT
TAKEGS

WHAT THE POLITICIAN DID WHEN HIS OPPONENT "LAID AN EGG."

Now arrange the circled letters to form the surprise answer, as suggested by the above cartoon.

Print answer here

PUZZLE
82

JUMBLE®

Unscramble these four Jumbles, one letter to each square, to form four ordinary words.

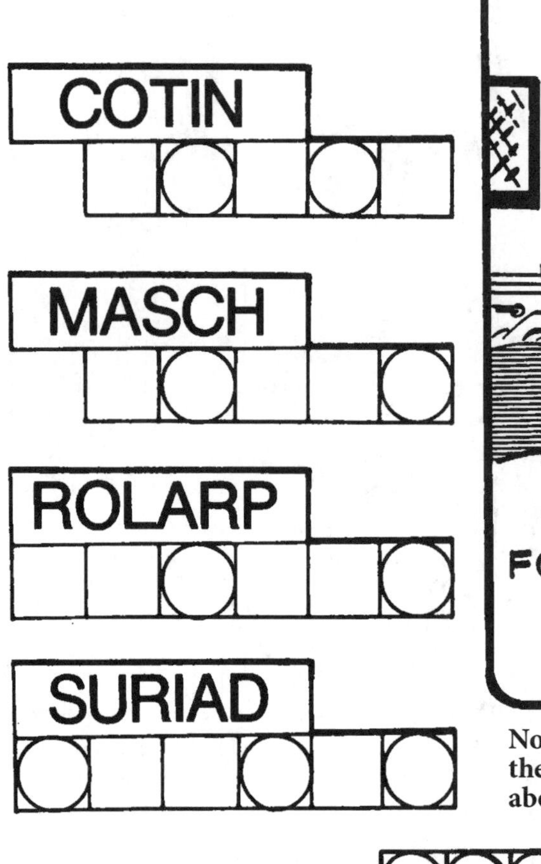
COTIN
MASCH
ROLARP
SURIAD

I know I'm going to hate the people there—I'm too good for them
THE EGOTIST FOUND FAULT WITH EVERYTHING EXCEPT THIS.

Now arrange the circled letters to form the surprise answer, as suggested by the above cartoon.

Print answer here

PUZZLE
83

JUMBLE®

Unscramble these four Jumbles, one letter to each square, to form four ordinary words.

LAUDT
VAHNE
YARNLE
FACEEF
You're getting it
DANCE
WHAT A GOOD DANCER HAS TO BE.

Now arrange the circled letters to form the surprise answer, as suggested by the above cartoon.

Print answer here " " WITH HIS

PUZZLE
84

JUMBLE®

Unscramble these four Jumbles, one letter to each square, to form four ordinary words.

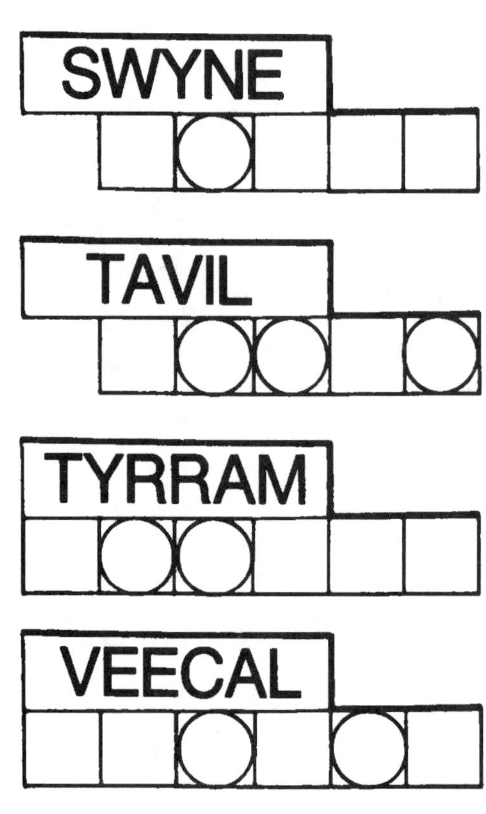
SWYNE
TAVIL
TYRRAM
VEECAL

DAD
SOME PEOPLE ARE RICHER THAN OTHERS– WHICH PROVES THAT WEALTH MAY BE ONLY THIS.

Now arrange the circled letters to form the surprise answer, as suggested by the above cartoon.

Print answer here " "

PUZZLE
85

JUMBLE®

Unscramble these four Jumbles, one letter to each square, to form four ordinary words.

MUTON

TOQUA

UNBRAU

AGCUTH

Somebody better put a stop to this or he's going to be sorry
THAT OFFENSIVE TALKER HAD A TONGUE SO SHARP HE ALMOST DID THIS.

Now arrange the circled letters to form the surprise answer, as suggested by the above cartoon.

Print answer here HIS OWN

PUZZLE
86

JUMBLE®

Unscramble these four Jumbles, one letter to each square, to form four ordinary words.

LIXEE
STRUY
TRAGEY
GARCHE
He left nothing but debts
WHAT THE SPEND-THRIFT ENDED UP MAKING.

Now arrange the circled letters to form the surprise answer, as suggested by the above cartoon.

Print answer here HIS "◯◯◯◯◯" TURN ◯◯◯◯

PUZZLE
87

JUMBLE®

Unscramble these four Jumbles, one letter to each square, to form four ordinary words.

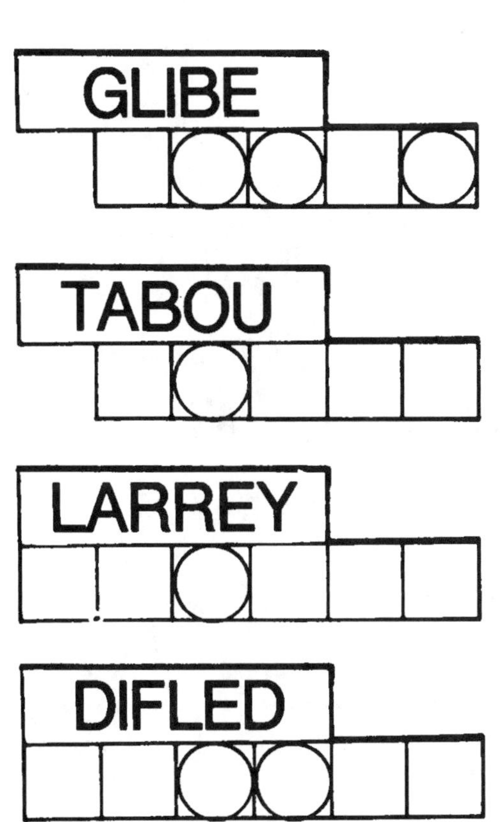

GLIBE
TABOU
LARREY
DIFLED

WHAT A MAN GIVEN TO HORSE-LAUGHS SHOULD BE.

Now arrange the circled letters to form the surprise answer, as suggested by the above cartoon.

Print answer here " "

PUZZLE
88

JUMBLE®

Unscramble these four Jumbles, one letter to each square, to form four ordinary words.

DOORE

NELIV

THYROW

AMMBLE

(Yawn) I'll take over, Dad
WHAT?!
$ $
HE OFFERED TO HELP WITH THE LAWN BECAUSE HE NEEDED THIS.

Now arrange the circled letters to form the surprise answer, as suggested by the above cartoon.

Print answer here " "

PUZZLE
89

JUMBLE®

Unscramble these four Jumbles, one letter to each square, to form four ordinary words.

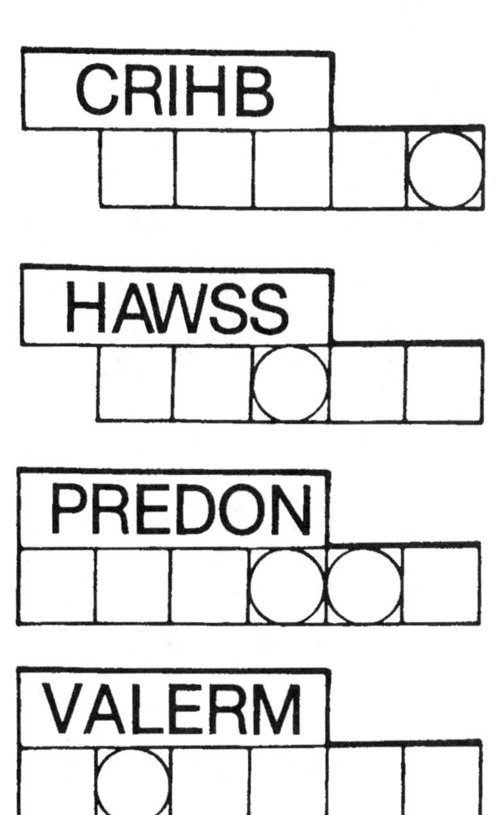
CRIHB
HAWSS
PREDON
VALERM

A WOMAN WITHOUT A HEART MIGHT MAKE A FOOL OF A MAN WITHOUT THIS.

Now arrange the circled letters to form the surprise answer, as suggested by the above cartoon.

Print answer here 

JUMBLE®

Unscramble these four Jumbles, one letter to each square, to form four ordinary words.

TIPEY

YICIL

RYTOLL

ALFFEB

Uh...er...
uh...
HIS INABILITY TO TELL THE TRUTH TURNED OUT TO BE THIS FOR HIM.

Now arrange the circled letters to form the surprise answer, as suggested by the above cartoon.

Print answer here A "◯◯◯-◯◯◯◯◯◯◯◯"

PUZZLE
91

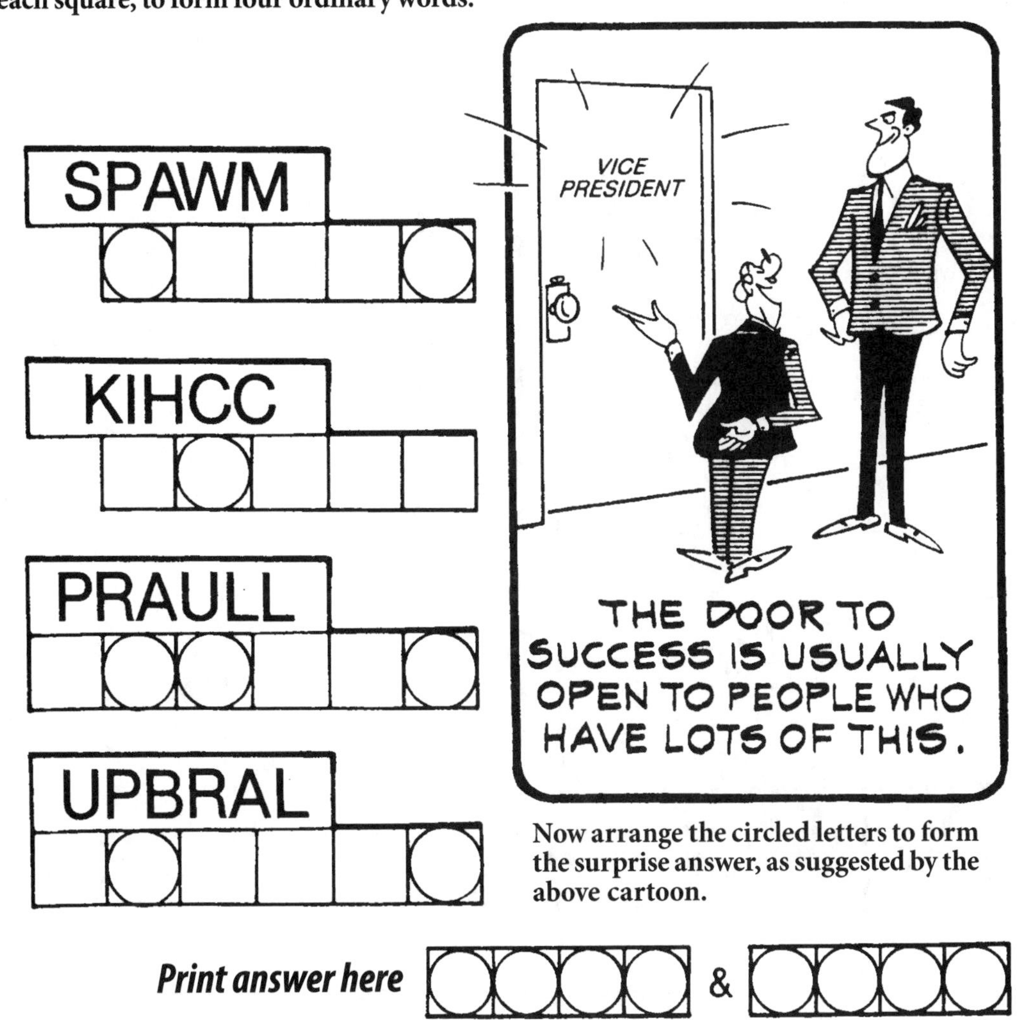

JUMBLE®
Unscramble these four Jumbles, one letter to each square, to form four ordinary words.
SPAWM
KIHCC
PRAULL
UPBRAL
VICE PRESIDENT
THE DOOR TO SUCCESS IS USUALLY OPEN TO PEOPLE WHO HAVE LOTS OF THIS.

Now arrange the circled letters to form the surprise answer, as suggested by the above cartoon.

Print answer here ☐☐☐☐ & ☐☐☐☐

PUZZLE
92

JUMBLE®

Unscramble these four Jumbles, one letter to each square, to form four ordinary words.

NAPOR
FECOR
POYNAC
ELCHEK
!
WHAT THAT ARROGANT INSECT WAS.

Now arrange the circled letters to form the surprise answer, as suggested by the above cartoon.

Print answer here A

PUZZLE
93

JUMBLE®

Unscramble these four Jumbles, one letter to each square, to form four ordinary words.

PUMIO
YIHFS
COSHUL
TIENNY
WHEN HE PROPOSED THAT THEY GET MARRIED, SHE TOLD HIM THAT THE OUTCOME WOULD DEPEND ON THIS.

Now arrange the circled letters to form the surprise answer, as suggested by the above cartoon.

Print answer here

PUZZLE
94

JUMBLE®

Unscramble these four Jumbles, one letter to each square, to form four ordinary words.

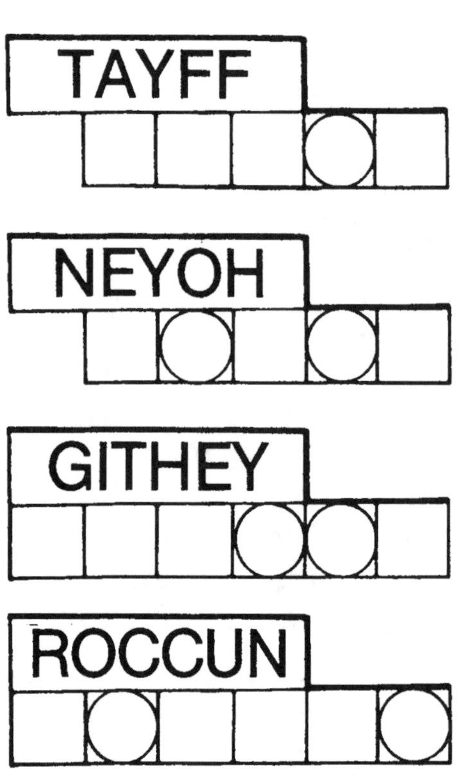
TAYFF
NEYOH
GITHEY
ROCCUN

YOU SHOW POISE WHEN YOU RAISE YOUR EYEBROWS INSTEAD OF THIS.

Now arrange the circled letters to form the surprise answer, as suggested by the above cartoon.

Print answer here

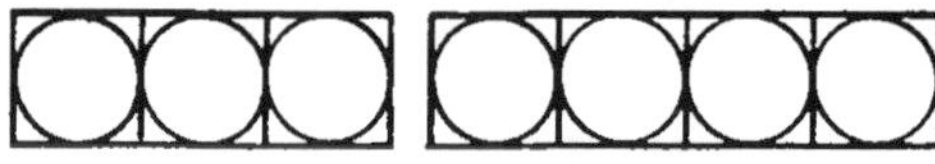

PUZZLE
95

JUMBLE®

Unscramble these four Jumbles, one letter to each square, to form four ordinary words.

GEMAL

YORFT

RULTSY

TUPPIL

IF YOUR "PANCAKE" MAKEUP ISN'T ALL YOU EXPECTED IT TO BE, YOU MIGHT TRY ADDING THIS.

Now arrange the circled letters to form the surprise answer, as suggested by the above cartoon.

Print answer here

PUZZLE
96

JUMBLE®

Unscramble these four Jumbles, one letter to each square, to form four ordinary words.

RIMEN
LANVA
GORNTS
ROOLIE
THE RIGHT TIME TO BUY A BOAT.

Now arrange the circled letters to form the surprise answer, as suggested by the above cartoon.

Print answer here WHEN THERE'S ◯ "◯◯◯◯" ◯◯ ◯◯

PUZZLE
97

JUMBLE®

Unscramble these four Jumbles, one letter to each square, to form four ordinary words.

KARAP
ELLIB
CAHBLE
DAYDEL
THE FORTUNE-TELLER SAID SHE LIKED HER WORK BECAUSE SHE ALWAYS DID THIS.
Now arrange the circled letters to form the surprise answer, as suggested by the above cartoon.
Print answer here
“ ”

PUZZLE
98

JUMBLE®

Unscramble these four Jumbles, one letter to each square, to form four ordinary words.

GANOW

COKAL

TALLYF

SURDIA

Wish I hadn't listened to my brother-in-law
You should have gone to a professional
THAT SO-CALLED FINANCIAL ADVISOR IS ALWAYS READY TO BACK HIS JUDG-MENT WITH THIS.

Now arrange the circled letters to form the surprise answer, as suggested by the above cartoon.

Print answer here YOUR

PUZZLE
99

JUMBLE®

Unscramble these four Jumbles, one letter to each square, to form four ordinary words.

NEFEC
TARFD
REPOPH
HERTHS
What a surprise!
IF SOMEONE IS NOW CELEBRATING HIS BIRTHDAY, THERE'S NO GIFT LIKE THIS.

Now arrange the circled letters to form the surprise answer, as suggested by the above cartoon.

Print answer here “ ”

PUZZLE
100

JUMBLE®

Unscramble these four Jumbles, one letter to each square, to form four ordinary words.

OPTIV
YOWND
TAYFUL
MOECEB
WHERE YOU MIGHT SEE A SHOOTING STAR.

Now arrange the circled letters to form the surprise answer, as suggested by the above cartoon.

Print answer here IN A

PUZZLE
101

JUMBLE®

Unscramble these four Jumbles, one letter to each square, to form four ordinary words.

BISSA
NEGIF
CORLLS
ROTTAH
I'm going home to Mother!
But all I said was...
JUST MARRIED
LOVE AT FIRST SIGHT SOMETIMES BREAKS UP AT---

Now arrange the circled letters to form the surprise answer, as suggested by the above cartoon.

Print answer here

PUZZLE
102

JUMBLE®

Unscramble these four Jumbles, one letter to each square, to form four ordinary words.

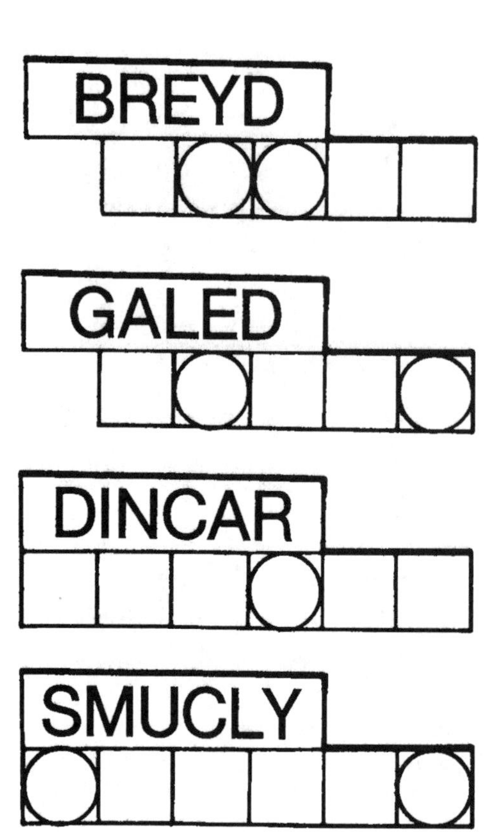
BREYD
GALED
DINCAR
SMUCLY

WHAT HE HOPED THIS EXERCISE WOULD DO TO HIS BODY FAT.

Now arrange the circled letters to form the surprise answer, as suggested by the above cartoon.

Print answer here

IT

PUZZLE
103

JUMBLE®

Unscramble these four Jumbles, one letter to each square, to form four ordinary words.

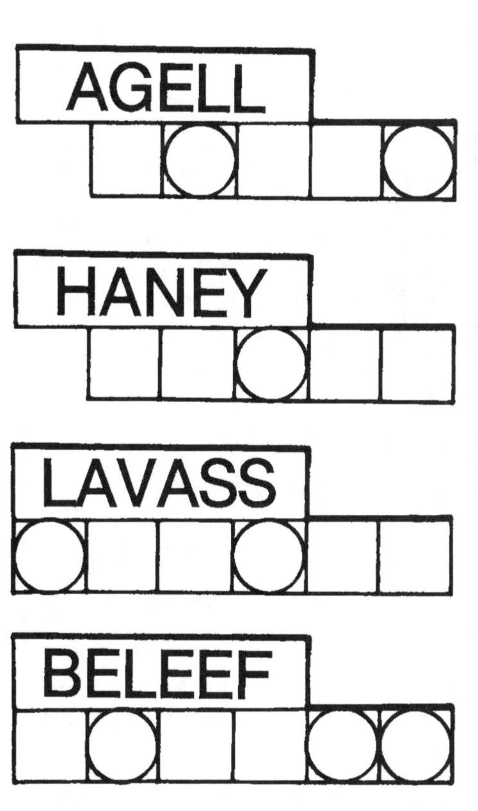
AGELL
HANEY
LAVASS
BELEEF

SOME FASHIONS
ARE CUT TO THIS.

Now arrange the circled letters to form the surprise answer, as suggested by the above cartoon.

Print answer here " " " "

PUZZLE
104

JUMBLE®

Unscramble these four Jumbles, one letter to each square, to form four ordinary words.

HESEP

ACTEX

WARROM

TRYDAW

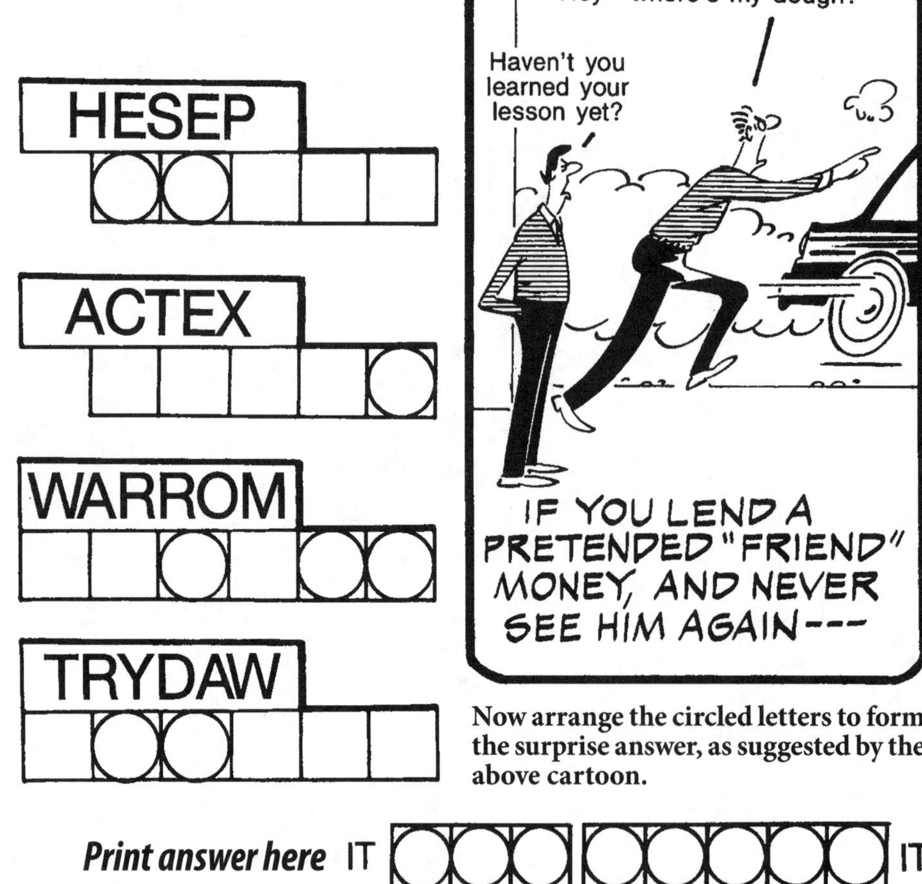
Hey--where's my dough?
Haven't you learned your lesson yet?
IF YOU LEND A PRETENDED "FRIEND" MONEY, AND NEVER SEE HIM AGAIN---

Now arrange the circled letters to form the surprise answer, as suggested by the above cartoon.

Print answer here IT ◯◯◯ ◯◯◯◯◯ IT

PUZZLE
105

JUMBLE®
Unscramble these four Jumbles, one letter to each square, to form four ordinary words.
STURY
ENVAH
GAIWHE
DOLFYN
WHAT THEY SAID TO THE NUT WHO CLAIMED TO HAVE INVENTED A NEW TYPE OF SIEVE.

Now arrange the circled letters to form the surprise answer, as suggested by the above cartoon.

Print answer here “THAT WON'T ◯◯◯◯◯ ◯◯◯◯◯◯”

PUZZLE
106

JUMBLE®

Unscramble these four Jumbles, one letter to each square, to form four ordinary words.

UPTYT

ROGIN

DEECIV

SCOMAT

I want you to meet some friends of mine. They don't have much money, but they're lots of fun
THE OPPORTUNIST HAS NO USE FOR FRIENDS---

Now arrange the circled letters to form the surprise answer, as suggested by the above cartoon.

Print answer here HE ___ ' _ " ___ "

PUZZLE
107

JUMBLE®

Unscramble these four Jumbles, one letter to each square, to form four ordinary words.

KADEB
TAFOO
RUMIAD
NIMERV
WHAT THE SAILOR SHOUTED WHEN HE SAW THE SURFER.
Now arrange the circled letters to form the surprise answer, as suggested by the above cartoon.
Print answer here
“ ”

JUMBLE®

Unscramble these four Jumbles, one letter to each square, to form four ordinary words.

TIELE

FYTHE

SPYNAP

DITORR

AT THE END OF THAT SHOPPING SPREE, SHE WAS---

Now arrange the circled letters to form the surprise answer, as suggested by the above cartoon.

Print answer here ☐☐☐☐☐ AS WELL AS "☐☐☐☐☐"

PUZZLE
109

JUMBLE®

Unscramble these four Jumbles, one letter to each square, to form four ordinary words.

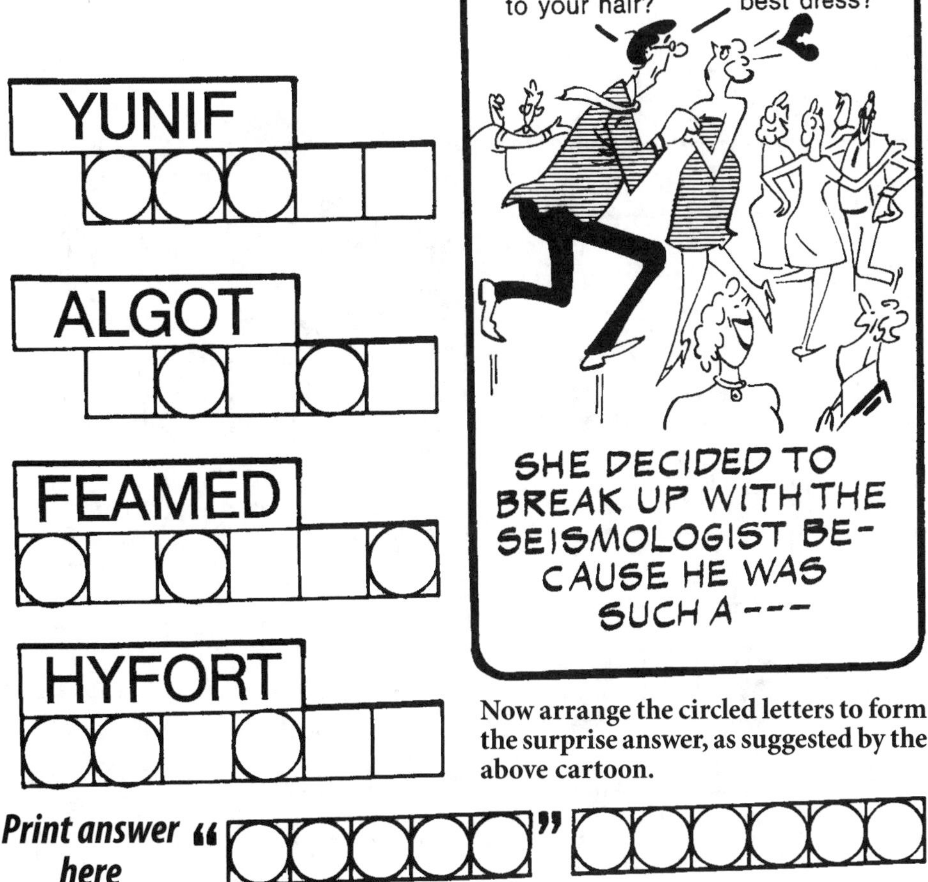
YUNIF
ALGOT
FEAMED
HYFORT
What happened to your hair?
Is that your best dress?
SHE DECIDED TO BREAK UP WITH THE SEISMOLOGIST BE-CAUSE HE WAS SUCH A ---
Print answer here

Now arrange the circled letters to form the surprise answer, as suggested by the above cartoon.

PUZZLE
110

JUMBLE®

Unscramble these four Jumbles, one letter to each square, to form four ordinary words.

HINSY

YAMOF

AIRFUN

COORTH

A RICH RELATIVE IS ALWAYS CLOSE TO YOU UNTIL YOU TRY TO---

Now arrange the circled letters to form the surprise answer, as suggested by the above cartoon.

Print answer here " ◯◯◯◯◯ " ◯◯◯

PUZZLE
111

JUMBLE®

Unscramble these four Jumbles, one letter to each square, to form four ordinary words.

ROGAC

HELEW

BRYDOW

ZARDAH

It wasn't easy
HOW THE MISER ACCUMULATED ALL THAT MONEY.

Now arrange the circled letters to form the surprise answer, as suggested by the above cartoon.

Print answer here THE " "

JUMBLE®

Unscramble these four Jumbles, one letter to each square, to form four ordinary words.

SHOIT

LANUN

WELLOY

THOTEG

Honest as the day is long
HE FOUND IT DIFFICULT TO STOOP---

Now arrange the circled letters to form the surprise answer, as suggested by the above cartoon.

Print answer here TO

PUZZLE
113

JUMBLE®

Unscramble these four Jumbles, one letter to each square, to form four ordinary words.

HURTT
REZIP
BRAMKE
TUGELL
Z
HE SEEMED TO BE SAWING WOOD IN HIS SLUMBER BECAUSE THIS WAS IN IT.

Now arrange the circled letters to form the surprise answer, as suggested by the above cartoon.

Print answer here " "

PUZZLE
114

JUMBLE®

Unscramble these four Jumbles, one letter to each square, to form four ordinary words.

ANCOP

DRAIP

MUDINS

LEMITY

Sure loves himself
E
WHAT THE EGOTIST WAS SUFFERING FROM.

Now arrange the circled letters to form the surprise answer, as suggested by the above cartoon.

Print answer here " "

PUZZLE
115

JUMBLE®

Unscramble these four Jumbles, one letter to each square, to form four ordinary words.

SYKAH
RODAH
IMVOTE
STEJER
WHAT THE CUTE LITTLE POTATO WAS WARNED AGAINST.

Now arrange the circled letters to form the surprise answer, as suggested by the above cartoon.

Print answer here

PUZZLE
116

JUMBLE®

Unscramble these four Jumbles, one letter to each square, to form four ordinary words.

YONIR

TOJUS

YONIFT

WURCEF

TAXES
WHAT THE CHIROPRACTOR AND HIS WIFE WERE WORKING ON.

Now arrange the circled letters to form the surprise answer, as suggested by the above cartoon.

Print answer here A

PUZZLE
117

JUMBLE®

Unscramble these four Jumbles, one letter to each square, to form four ordinary words.

SOMYS
RUGPO
GORUME
THEIRE
WHAT BOARDING HOUSE GOSSIP USED TO START WITH.

Now arrange the circled letters to form the surprise answer, as suggested by the above cartoon.

Print answer here " "

PUZZLE
118

JUMBLE®

Unscramble these four Jumbles, one letter to each square, to form four ordinary words.

ASOBS
MORRA
KALTEC
CUSTOC
WHAT THE TWELVE BOTTLES OF MOONSHINE EVENTUALLY BECAME.

Now arrange the circled letters to form the surprise answer, as suggested by the above cartoon.

Print answer here A

PUZZLE
119

JUMBLE®

Unscramble these four Jumbles, one letter to each square, to form four ordinary words.

STYTA

MIRPE

HUNGOE

DESAUB

Couldn't care less
Z
Z
WORLD IN A MESS
WHAT YOU MIGHT GET FROM A *SENATOR*.

Now arrange the circled letters to form the surprise answer, as suggested by the above cartoon.

Print answer here " ◯◯ ◯◯◯◯◯ "

PUZZLE
120

JUMBLE®

Unscramble these four Jumbles, one letter to each square, to form four ordinary words.

GUFED
SIVAT
CUDLAN
CEETIN
RATHER BIG FOR BALLET THESE DAYS.
Now arrange the circled letters to form the surprise answer, as suggested by the above cartoon.
Print answer here

PUZZLE
121

JUMBLE®

Unscramble these four Jumbles, one letter to each square, to form four ordinary words.

VOYCE

WETHA

YEKTUR

COZADI

They'll never clean that up
WHAT HAPPENED WHEN THE GARBAGE TRUCK OVERTURNED.

Now arrange the circled letters to form the surprise answer, as suggested by the above cartoon.

Print answer here IT "⬜⬜⬜⬜⬜⬜" ⬜⬜⬜⬜⬜

PUZZLE
122

JUMBLE®

Unscramble these four Jumbles, one letter to each square, to form four ordinary words.

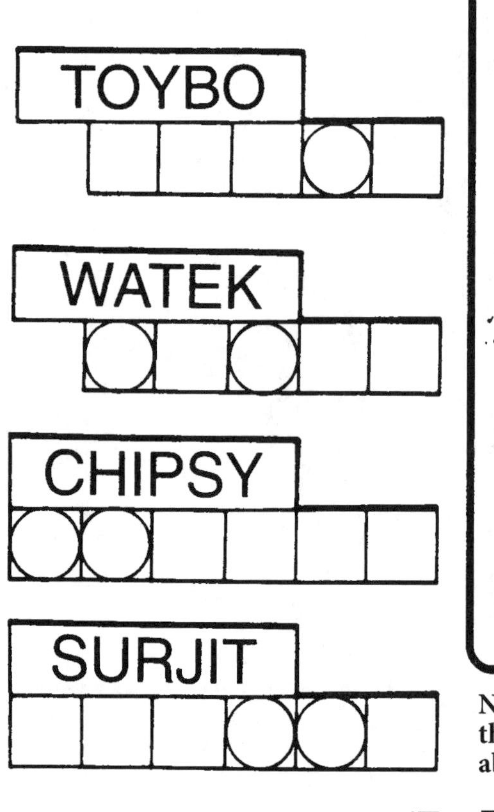
TOYBO
WATEK
CHIPSY
SURJIT

Next, we've got to clean 'em
WHY THE CHERRY PICKER DISLIKED HIS JOB.

Now arrange the circled letters to form the surprise answer, as suggested by the above cartoon.

Print answer here IT WAS 

PUZZLE
123

JUMBLE®

Unscramble these four Jumbles, one letter to each square, to form four ordinary words.

KEREC
TABBO
KINNAP
FLOUND
WHAT THE BALD PRODUCE PEDDLER ENDED UP WITH.
Now arrange the circled letters to form the surprise answer, as suggested by the above cartoon.
Print answer here A

PUZZLE
124

JUMBLE®

Unscramble these four Jumbles, one letter to each square, to form four ordinary words.

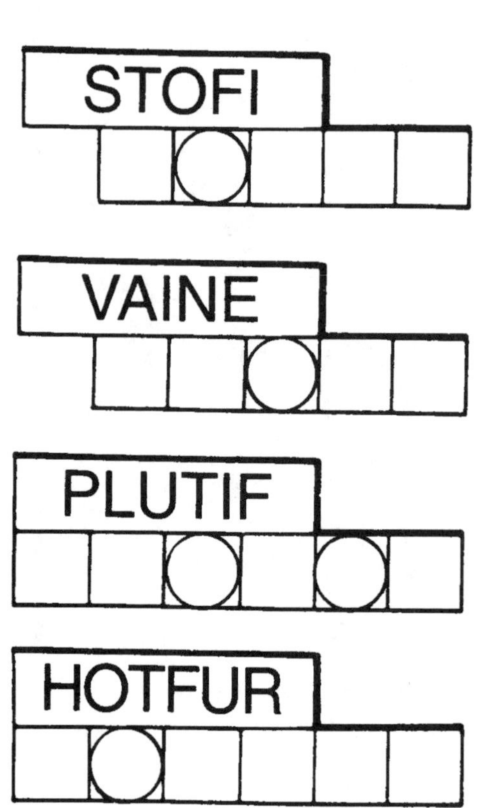
STOFI
VAINE
PLUTIF
HOTFUR

I'm gorgeous
THE EGOTISTICAL BEAUTY QUEEN WAS—

Now arrange the circled letters to form the surprise answer, as suggested by the above cartoon.

Print answer here AN  

PUZZLE
125

JUMBLE®

Unscramble these four Jumbles, one letter to each square, to form four ordinary words.

RAYRA

BIBAR

DINTAB

BRILEM

He sure knows his stuff
But he's a kook
ANOTHER NAME FOR THIS ORNITHOLOGIST.

Now arrange the circled letters to form the surprise answer, as suggested by the above cartoon.

Print answer here A

PUZZLE
126

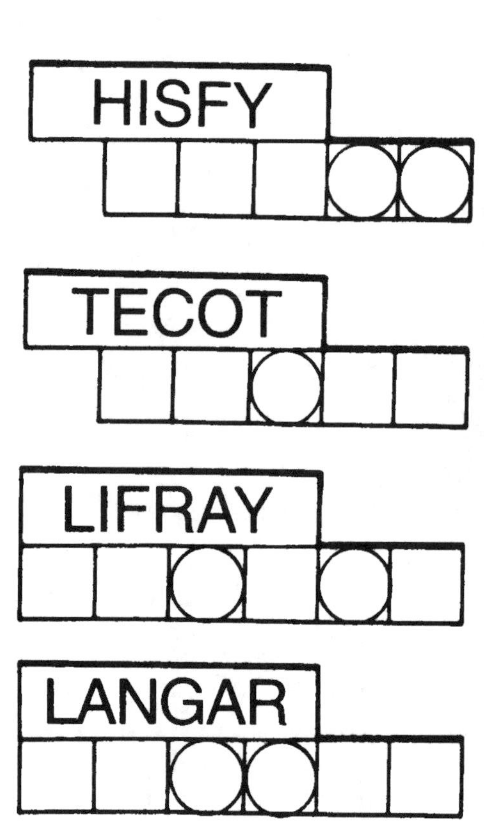
JUMBLE®
Unscramble these four Jumbles, one letter to each square, to form four ordinary words.
HISFY
TECOT
LIFRAY
LANGAR

This is fun
1-25
HOW THE ELEC-TRICIAN'S HELPER TREATED HIS WORK.

Now arrange the circled letters to form the surprise answer, as suggested by the above cartoon.

Print answer here "  "

PUZZLE
127

JUMBLE®

Unscramble these four Jumbles, one letter to each square, to form four ordinary words.

TOBEG
TROOB
DABALL
EVITLY
HOW THE BOXER BECAME THE CHAMP.

Now arrange the circled letters to form the surprise answer, as suggested by the above cartoon.

Print answer here WITH A

PUZZLE
128

JUMBLE®

Unscramble these four Jumbles, one letter to each square, to form four ordinary words.

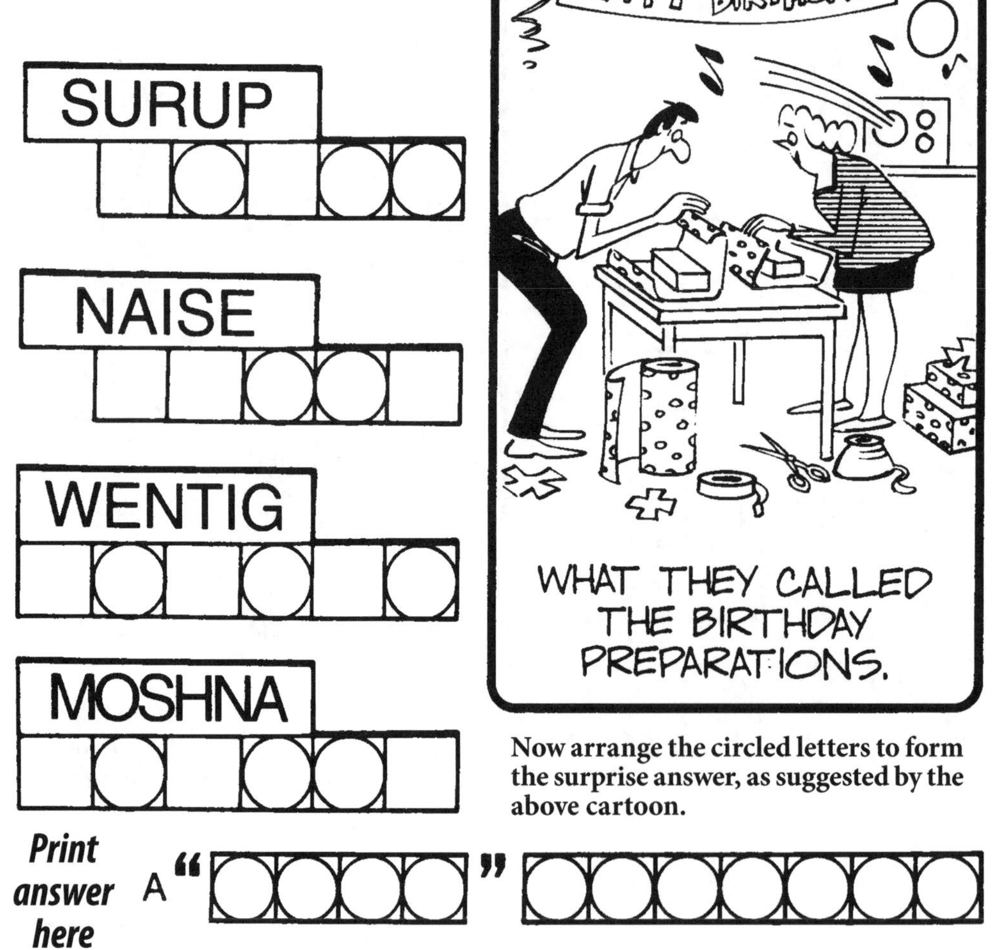
SURUP
NAISE
WENTIG
MOSHNA
HAPPY BIRTHDAY
WHAT THEY CALLED THE BIRTHDAY PREPARATIONS.
Now arrange the circled letters to form the surprise answer, as suggested by the above cartoon.
Print answer here
A " "

PUZZLE
129

JUMBLE®

Unscramble these four Jumbles, one letter to each square, to form four ordinary words.

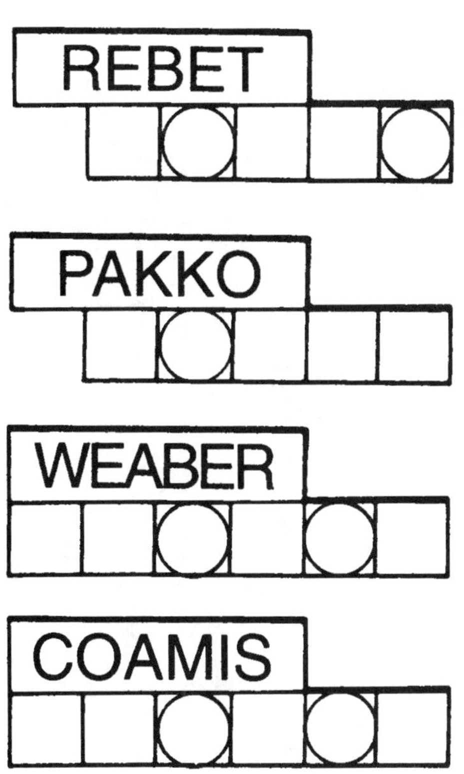
REBET
PAKKO
WEABER
COAMIS

Think we'll ever be served?
Hey — what's holding up our food?
WHAT THE PATRONS OF THE RESTAURANT BECAME.

Now arrange the circled letters to form the surprise answer, as suggested by the above cartoon.

Print answer here “”

PUZZLE
130

JUMBLE®

Unscramble these four Jumbles, one letter to each square, to form four ordinary words.

RASCY
TILEE
YARMID
RONACE
They're shorter this year
IN ONE YEAR AND OUT THE OTHER.

Now arrange the circled letters to form the surprise answer, as suggested by the above cartoon.

Print answer here

PUZZLE
131

JUMBLE®

Unscramble these four Jumbles, one letter to each square, to form four ordinary words.

ENDUC

COPUH

DANDIG

SUNEER

This clock was owned by President Coolidge!
It still works.
All Clocks 60% Off Today
ALL THE CLOCKS AT THE ANTIQUE CLOCK STORE WERE THIS.

Now arrange the circled letters to form the surprise answer, as suggested by the above cartoon.

Print answer here

PUZZLE
132

JUMBLE®

Unscramble these four Jumbles, one letter to each square, to form four ordinary words.

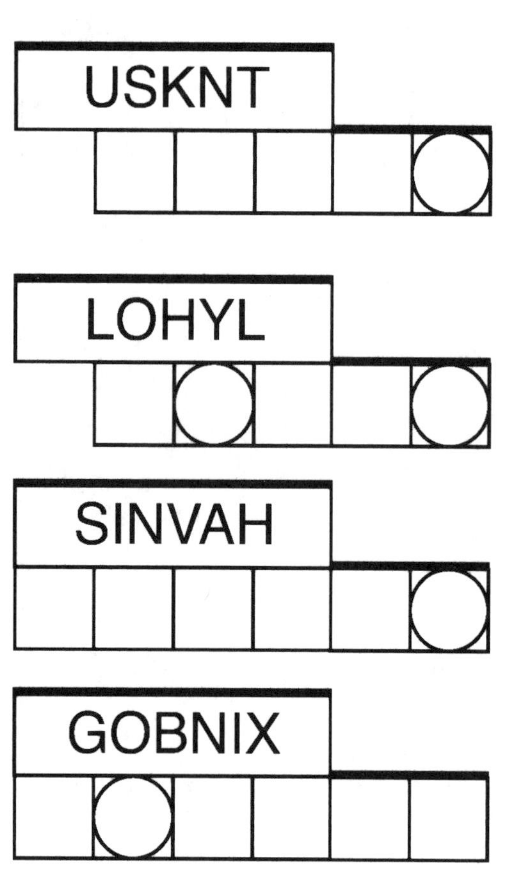
USKNT
LOHYL
SINVAH
GOBNIX

Has anyone seen Mr. Bueller?
STUDY HALL 3RD. PERIOD QUIET PLEASE
YOU CAN'T PLAY THIS IN SCHOOL.

Now arrange the circled letters to form the surprise answer, as suggested by the above cartoon.

Print answer here

PUZZLE
133

JUMBLE®

Unscramble these four Jumbles, one letter to each square, to form four ordinary words.

YODOZ

ULPEM

TRIBTE

SLUVIA

OK, class. What is A plus B plus C...No...I mean what is A and B divided by ten...No, wait...That's not right.
(a + b)^1 = a + b
(a + b)^2 = a^2 + 2ab + b^2
THE NEW MATH TEACHER WAS HAVING ---

Now arrange the circled letters to form the surprise answer, as suggested by the above cartoon.

Print answer here

PUZZLE
134

JUMBLE®

Unscramble these four Jumbles, one letter to each square, to form four ordinary words.

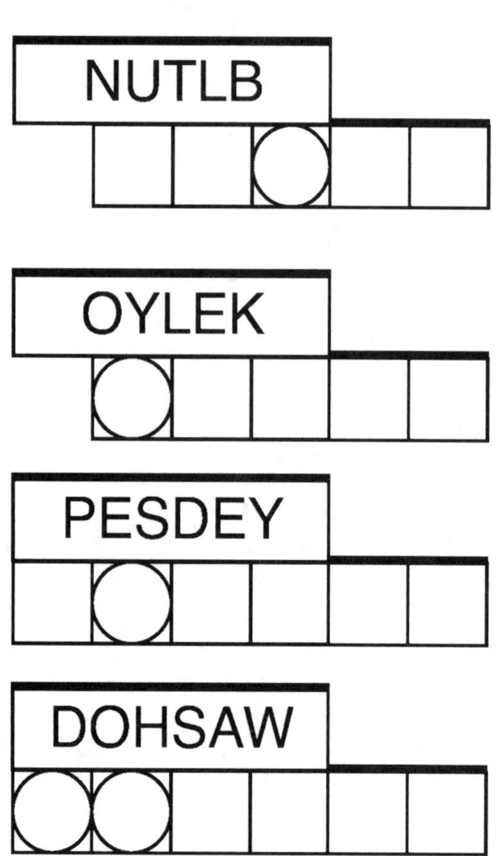
NUTLB
OYLEK
PESDEY
DOHSAW

I said, you really need a hot dog. You look hungry.
And I told you, I'm not hungry! Leave me alone.
SHE THOUGHT THE STREET VENDOR WAS ----

Now arrange the circled letters to form the surprise answer, as suggested by the above cartoon.

Print answer here

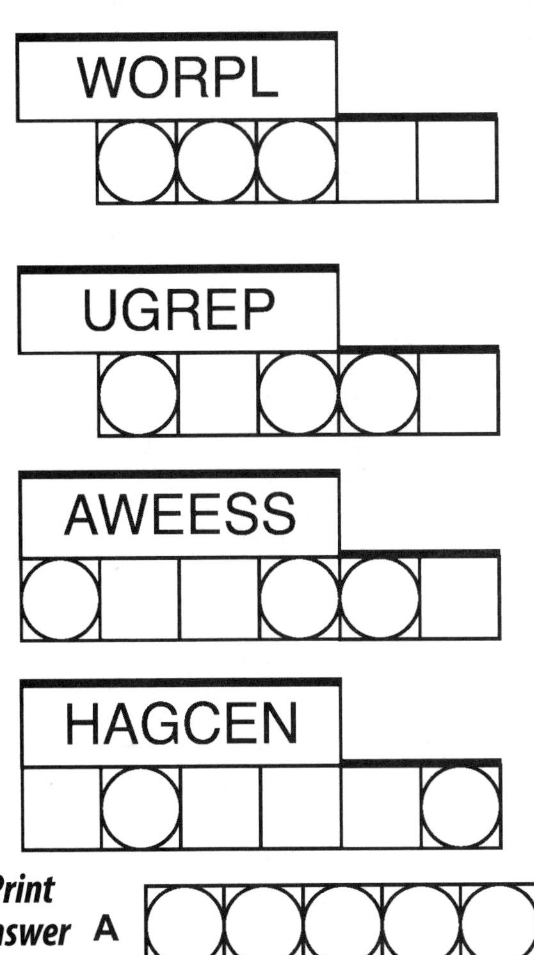
JUMBLE
Unscramble these four Jumbles, one letter to each square, to form four ordinary words.
WORPL
UGREP
AWEESS
HAGCEN

How did he get into our yard?
Oh, no! He's eating my flowers.
He's so cute!
WHAT DO YOU CALL A RABBIT ON THE LAWN?

Now arrange the circled letters to form the surprise answer, as suggested by the above cartoon.

Print answer here A

PUZZLE
136

JUMBLE®

Unscramble these four Jumbles, one letter to each square, to form four ordinary words.

NURPE

DPUPE

RIPTEM

SUEERM

In conclusion, when adding numbers, it's sometimes necessary to carry the 1.
1
121
+219
340
1
136
+482
618
WHEN THE MATH TEACHER ENDED THE LESSON, SHE ---

Now arrange the circled letters to form the surprise answer, as suggested by the above cartoon.

Print answer here

PUZZLE
137

JUMBLE®

Unscramble these four Jumbles, one letter to each square, to form four ordinary words.

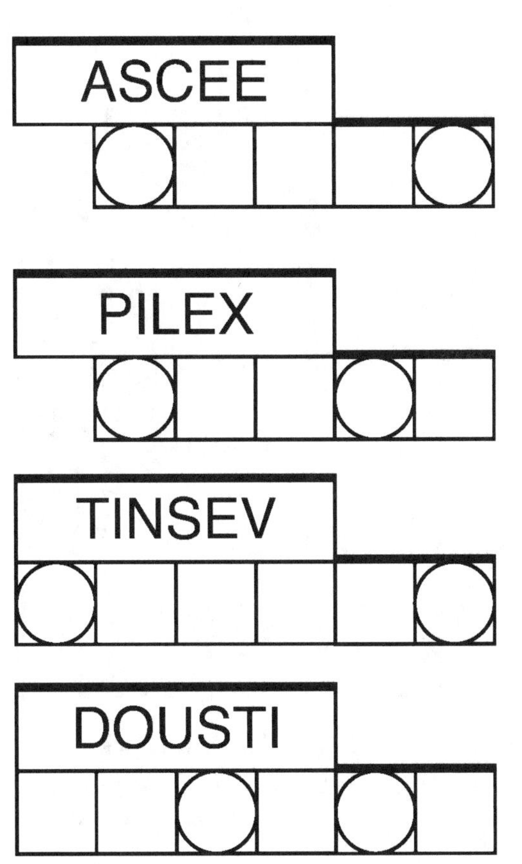
ASCEE
PILEX
TINSEV
DOUSTI

She is sweet! I'm going to ask her out.
Well, aren't you nice! This looks delicious.
Here you go, Ma'am.
THE NEW EMPLOYEE AT THE BAKERY WAS ---

Now arrange the circled letters to form the surprise answer, as suggested by the above cartoon.

Print answer here A  

PUZZLE
138

JUMBLE®

Unscramble these four Jumbles, one letter to each square, to form four ordinary words.

RYTID
LENKT
BERNKO
MAHFOT
My thought was that we don't use wheels. We use a belt of metal instead.
WHEN DEVELOPING A NEW ARMORED MILITARY VEHICLE DURING WORLD WAR ONE, THEY FORMED A ---

Now arrange the circled letters to form the surprise answer, as suggested by the above cartoon.

Print answer here

PUZZLE
139

JUMBLE®

Unscramble these four Jumbles, one letter to each square, to form four ordinary words.

LADYM

DUFIL

LUPLAR

ONEGXY

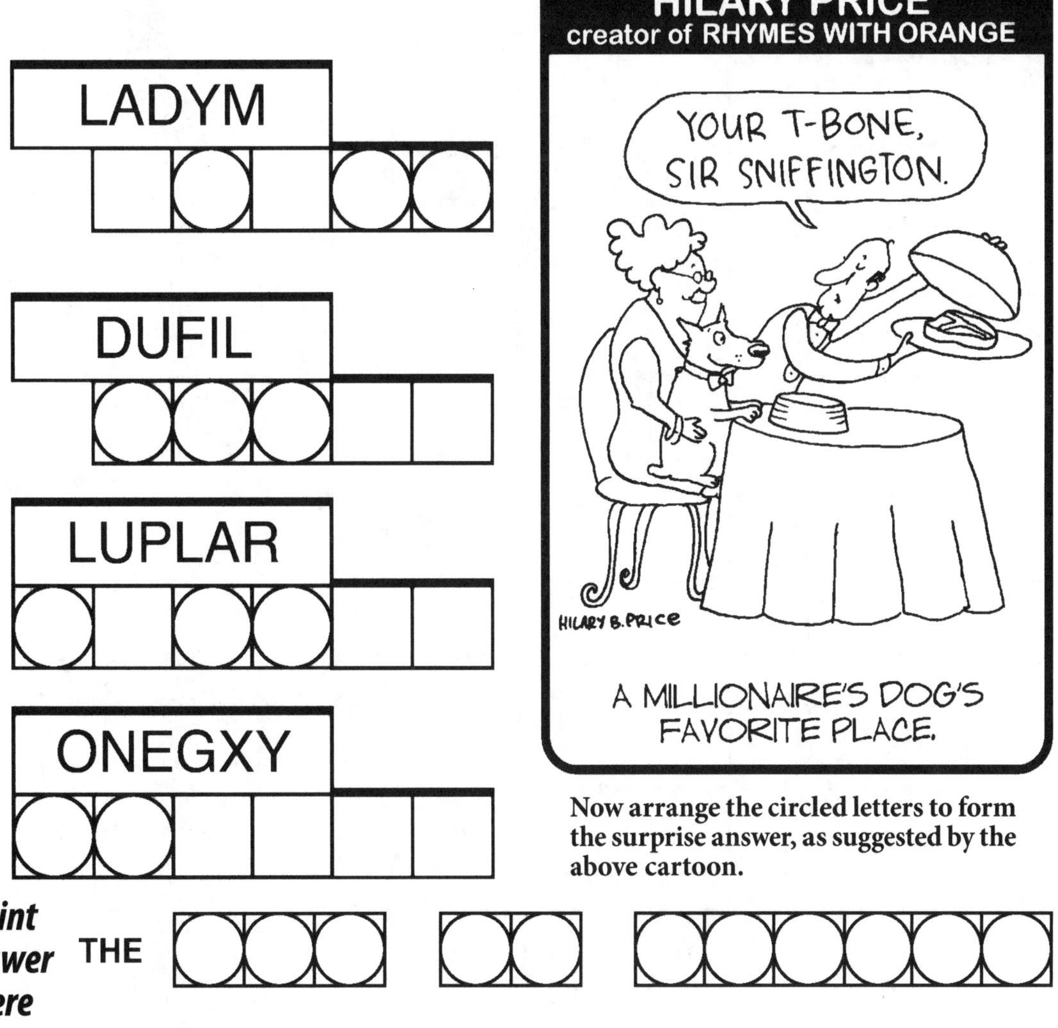
Today's Guest JUMBLER is
HILARY PRICE
creator of RHYMES WITH ORANGE
YOUR T-BONE,
SIR SNIFFINGTON.
HILARY B. PRICE
A MILLIONAIRE'S DOG'S
FAVORITE PLACE.

Now arrange the circled letters to form the surprise answer, as suggested by the above cartoon.

Print answer here THE

JUMBLE®

Unscramble these four Jumbles, one letter to each square, to form four ordinary words.

NOORH

TGIFH

SUNEAA

MOSTOH

Today's Guest JUMBLER is
JEFF KEANE
creator of THE FAMILY CIRCUS
GETS OFF SCHOOL BUS.
ARE YOU FEELING ALL RIGHT?
JEFF KEANE
MOMMY KNEW SOMETHING WAS WRONG BECAUSE BILLY CAME ---

Now arrange the circled letters to form the surprise answer, as suggested by the above cartoon.

Print answer here

PUZZLE
141

JUMBLE®

Unscramble these four Jumbles, one letter to each square, to form four ordinary words.

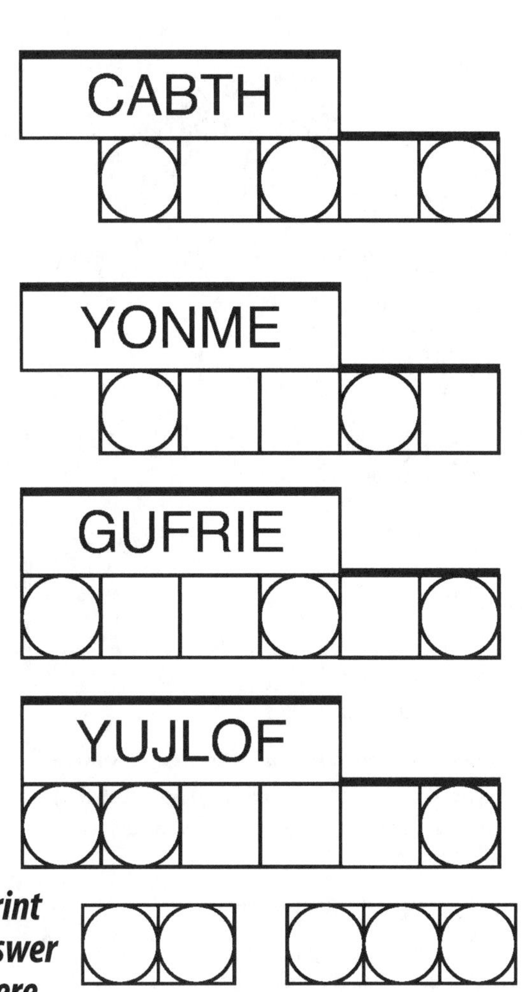
CABTH
YONME
GUFRIE
YUJLOF

Today's Guest JUMBLER is
DAVE COVERLY
creator of SPEED BUMP
COVERLY
WHEN A LION IS GREAT AT WORD PUZZLES, HE'S KNOWN AS "KING —— ."

Now arrange the circled letters to form the surprise answer, as suggested by the above cartoon.

Print answer here ”

PUZZLE
142

JUMBLE®

Unscramble these four Jumbles, one letter to each square, to form four ordinary words.

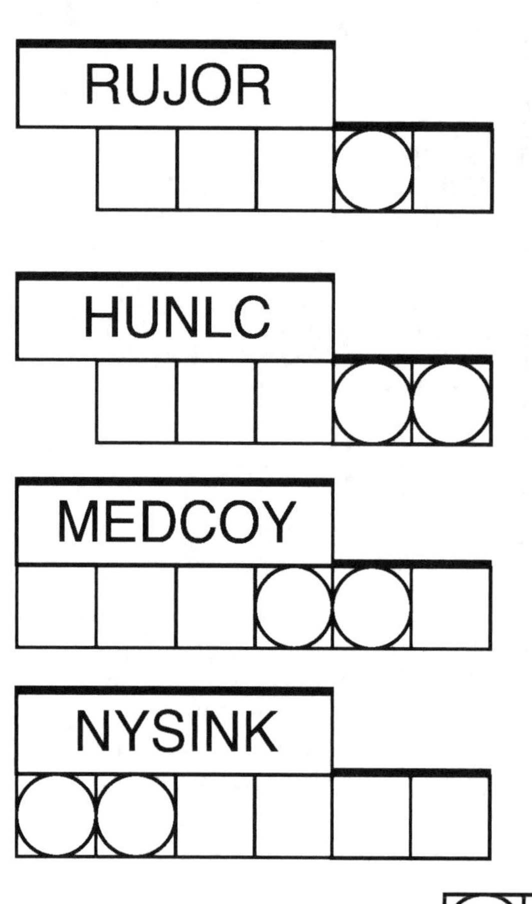
RUJOR
HUNLC
MEDCOY
NYSINK

Here you go. I broke it down to parts, labor and gratuity.
What! This costs more than my truck!
AFTER GETTING THE BILL FOR HIS TRUCK'S NEW SUSPENSION SYSTEM, HE WAS ---

Now arrange the circled letters to form the surprise answer, as suggested by the above cartoon.

Print answer here 

PUZZLE
143

JUMBLE®

Unscramble these four Jumbles, one letter to each square, to form four ordinary words.

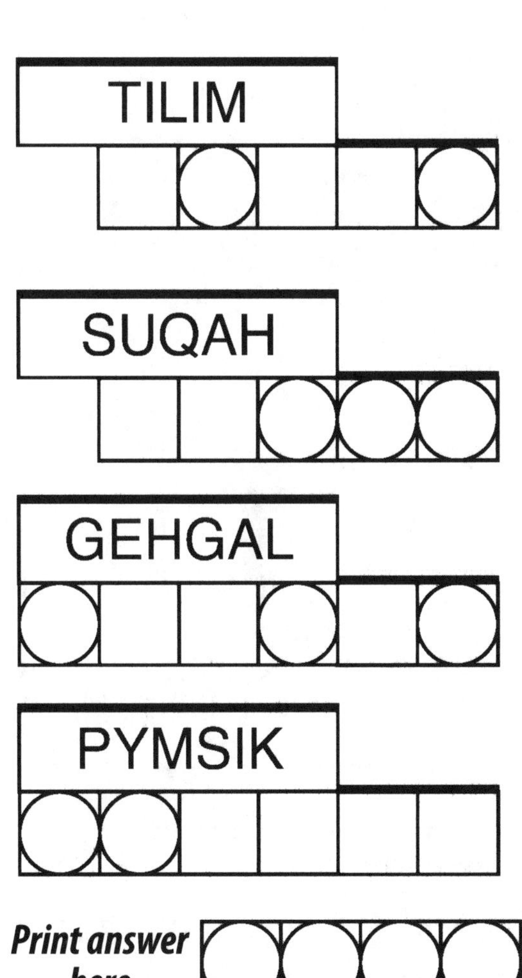
TILIM
SUQAH
GEHGAL
PYMSIK

$100,000 PER HAND BLACKJACK TOURNAMENT
I love the view from up here.
Luckily, it's not cloudy today.
THE MOUNTAINTOP CASINO FEATURED ---

Now arrange the circled letters to form the surprise answer, as suggested by the above cartoon.

Print answer here

PUZZLE
144

JUMBLE®

Unscramble these four Jumbles, one letter to each square, to form four ordinary words.

FRADT
NAYEH
SORMEK
LUPTIP

XXX// 250
X/X/ 241
THE FINALE OF THE BOWLING TOURNAMENT WAS SO EXCITING THAT YOU COULD ---

Now arrange the circled letters to form the surprise answer, as suggested by the above cartoon.

Print answer here

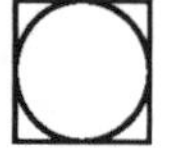

PUZZLE
145

JUMBLE®

Unscramble these four Jumbles, one letter to each square, to form four ordinary words.

MULPB

HUBMT

TENCIE

RADNOG

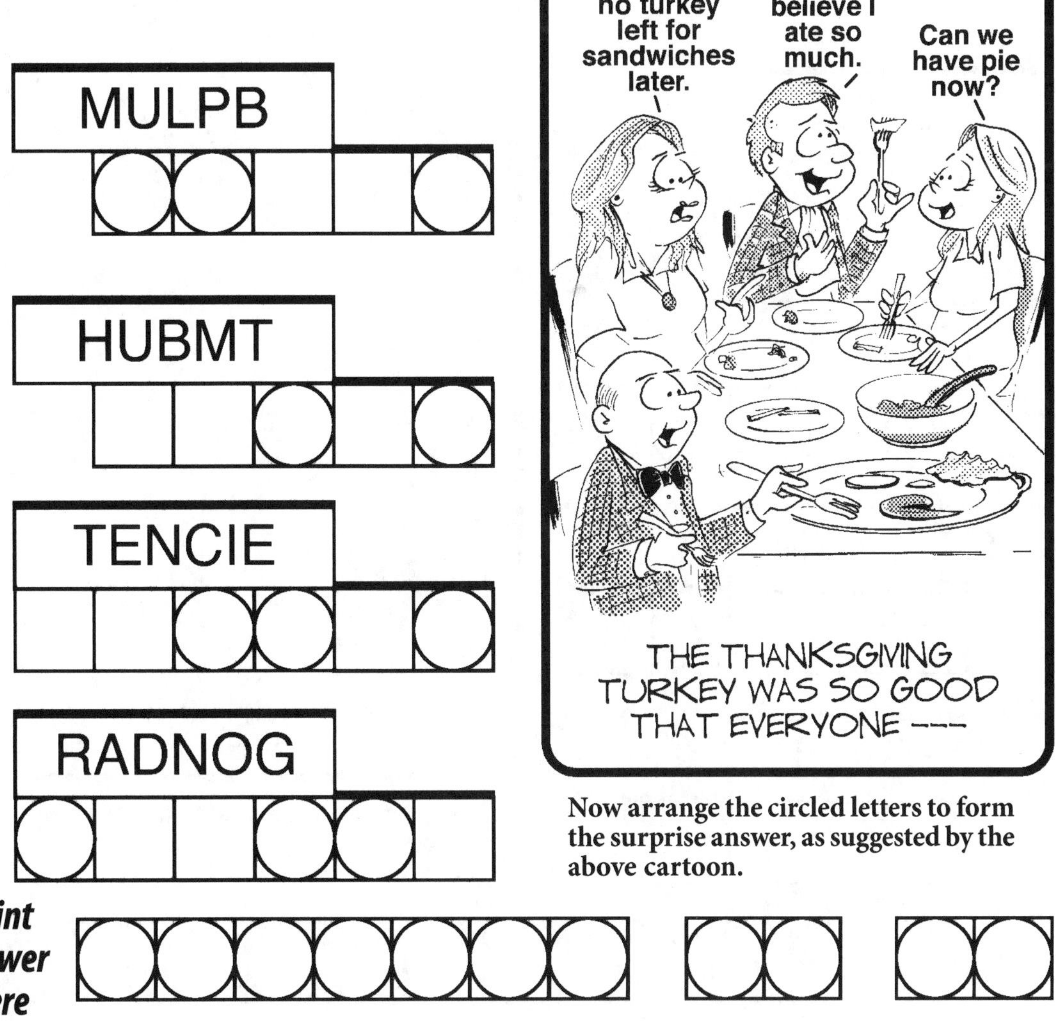
Aw! There's no turkey left for sandwiches later.
I can't believe I ate so much.
Can we have pie now?
THE THANKSGIVING TURKEY WAS SO GOOD THAT EVERYONE ---

Now arrange the circled letters to form the surprise answer, as suggested by the above cartoon.

Print answer here

PUZZLE
146

JUMBLE®

Unscramble these four Jumbles, one letter to each square, to form four ordinary words.

DUPEP

HATSS

ONTAAS

WESASE

Your grades stink, guys! You need to study more!
THE OCEANOGRAPHY CLASS CONSISTED OF ---

Now arrange the circled letters to form the surprise answer, as suggested by the above cartoon.

Print answer here " "

PUZZLE
147

JUMBLE®

Unscramble these four Jumbles, one letter to each square, to form four ordinary words.

MULAQ

VELLE

NATLEG

RICNOM

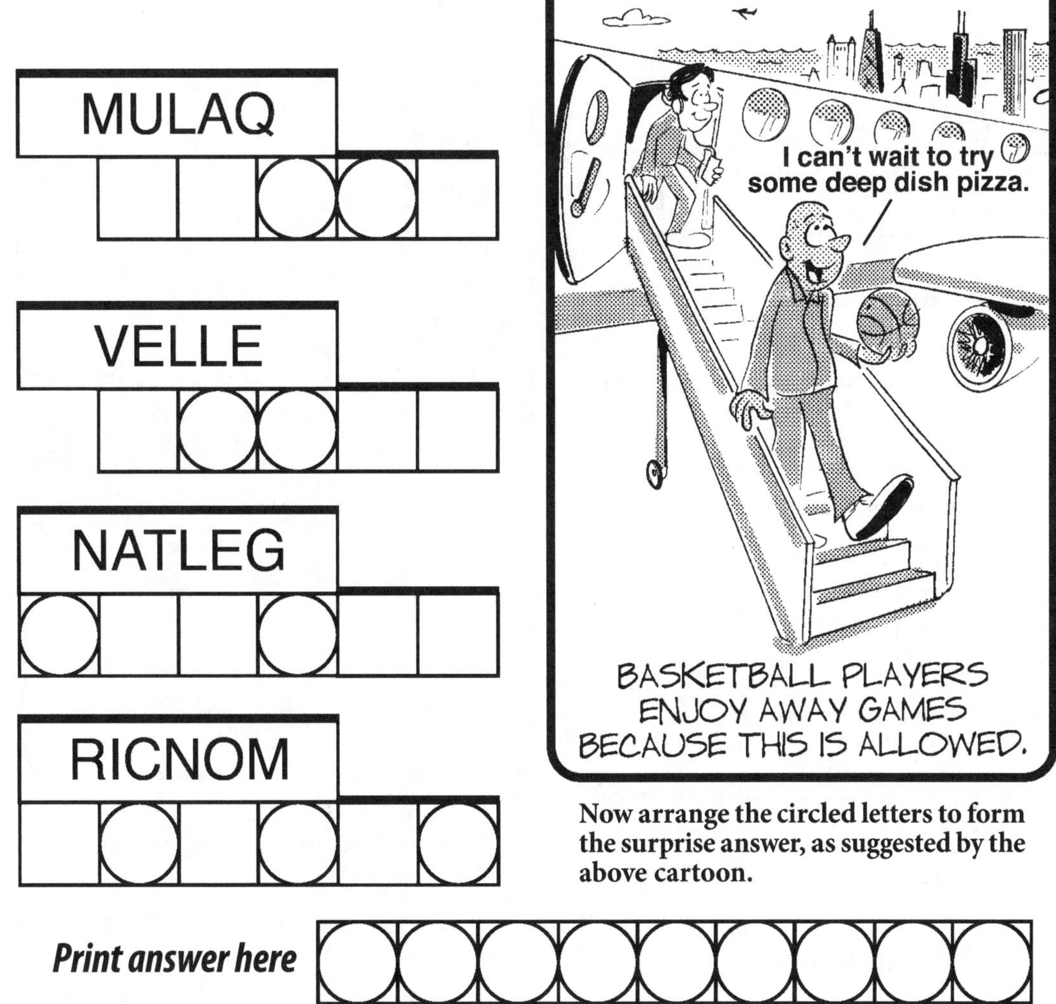
I can't wait to try some deep dish pizza.
BASKETBALL PLAYERS ENJOY AWAY GAMES BECAUSE THIS IS ALLOWED.

Now arrange the circled letters to form the surprise answer, as suggested by the above cartoon.

Print answer here

PUZZLE
148

JUMBLE®

Unscramble these four Jumbles, one letter to each square, to form four ordinary words.

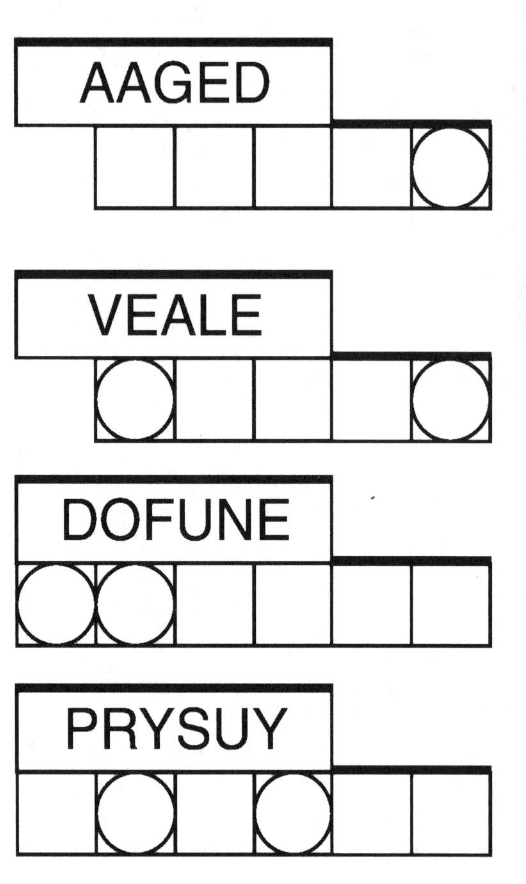
AAGED
VEALE
DOFUNE
PRYSUY

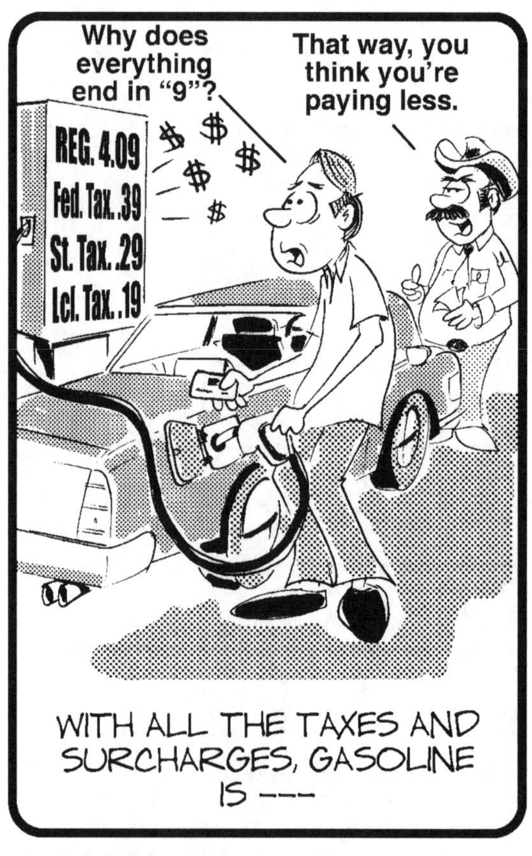
Why does everything end in "9"?
That way, you think you're paying less.
REG. 4.09
Fed. Tax .39
St. Tax .29
Lcl. Tax .19
WITH ALL THE TAXES AND SURCHARGES, GASOLINE IS ---

Now arrange the circled letters to form the surprise answer, as suggested by the above cartoon.

Print answer here "◯◯◯-◯◯◯-◯"

PUZZLE
149

JUMBLE®

Unscramble these four Jumbles, one letter to each square, to form four ordinary words.

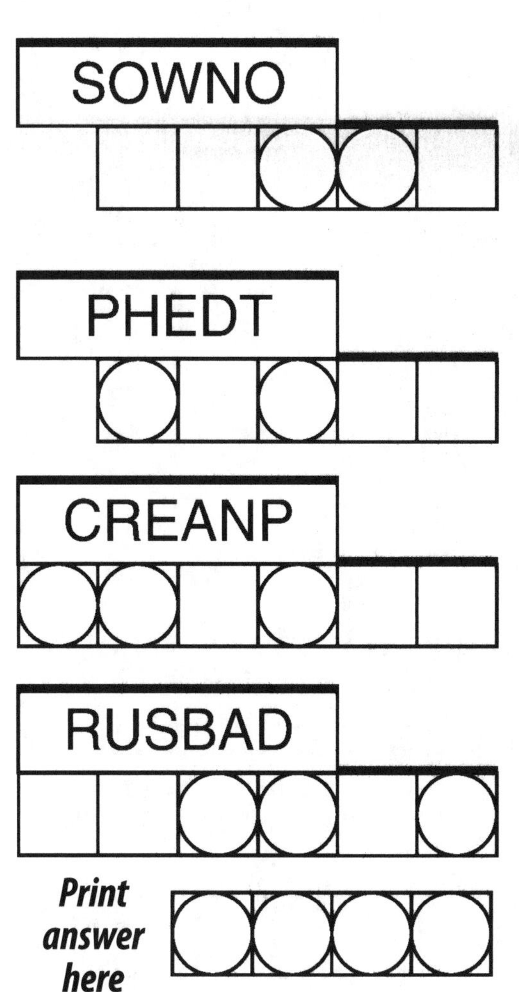
SOWNO
PHEDT
CREANP
RUSBAD
Print answer here

All you can eat! Challenge accepted.
Your doctor told you to knock off. This place is not going to help your diet.
ALL YOU CAN EAT
PICKING UP FOOD CAN MAKE IT HARD TO ---

Now arrange the circled letters to form the surprise answer, as suggested by the above cartoon.

PUZZLE
150

JUMBLE®

Unscramble these four Jumbles, one letter to each square, to form four ordinary words.

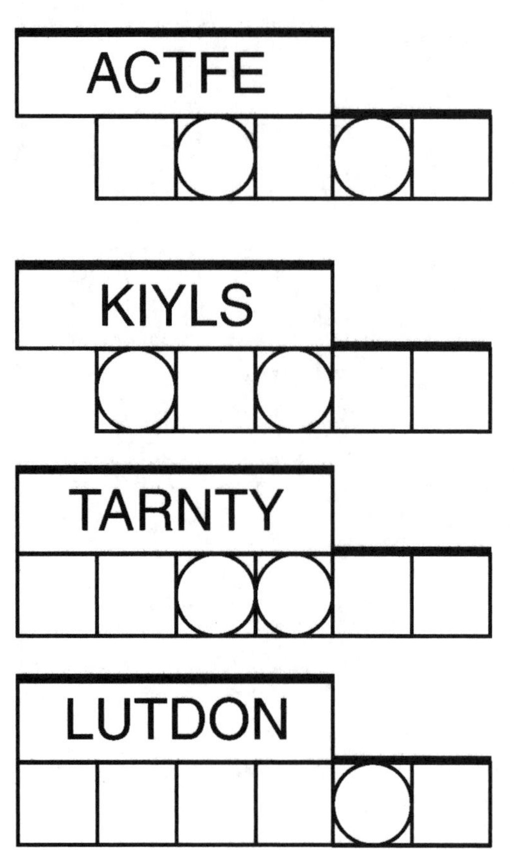
ACTFE
KIYLS
TARNTY
LUTDON

I had lunch with Daisy. She and Donald are having problems. Seems he has serious anger issues.
Really? Tell me more.
MINNIE MOUSE WAS TELLING MICKEY ABOUT HER DAY, AND MICKEY WAS ---

Now arrange the circled letters to form the surprise answer, as suggested by the above cartoon.

Print answer here

PUZZLE
151

JUMBLE®

Unscramble these four Jumbles, one letter to each square, to form four ordinary words.

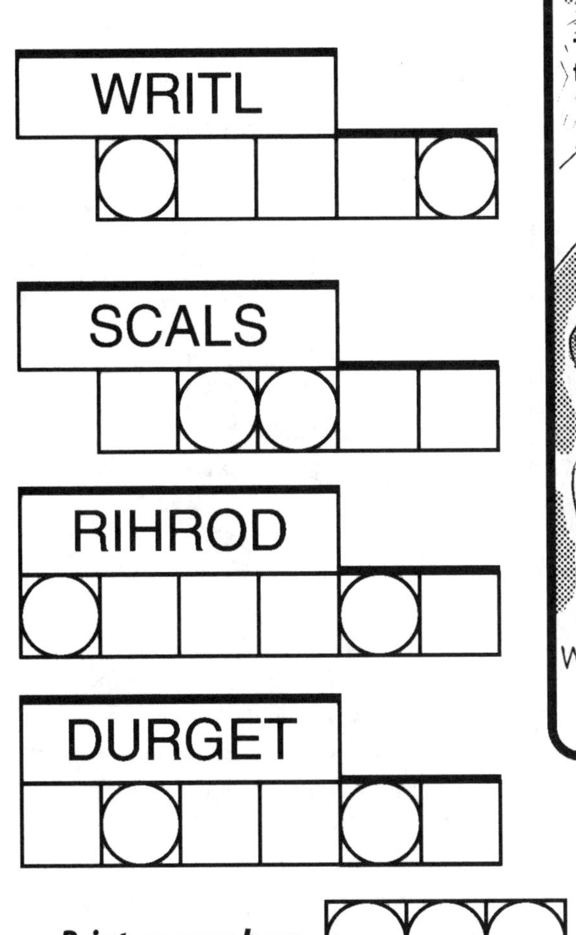
WRITL
SCALS
RIHROD
DURGET

This is going to take some getting used to.
I think it will be fine.
WHEN THEY TOLD THEM THEY'D BE DRIVING CLOCKWISE, THE DRIVERS SAID —

Now arrange the circled letters to form the surprise answer, as suggested by the above cartoon.

Print answer here  

PUZZLE
152

JUMBLE®

Unscramble these four Jumbles, one letter to each square, to form four ordinary words.

HBMUT

DUNWO

BOLGON

MRYFIL

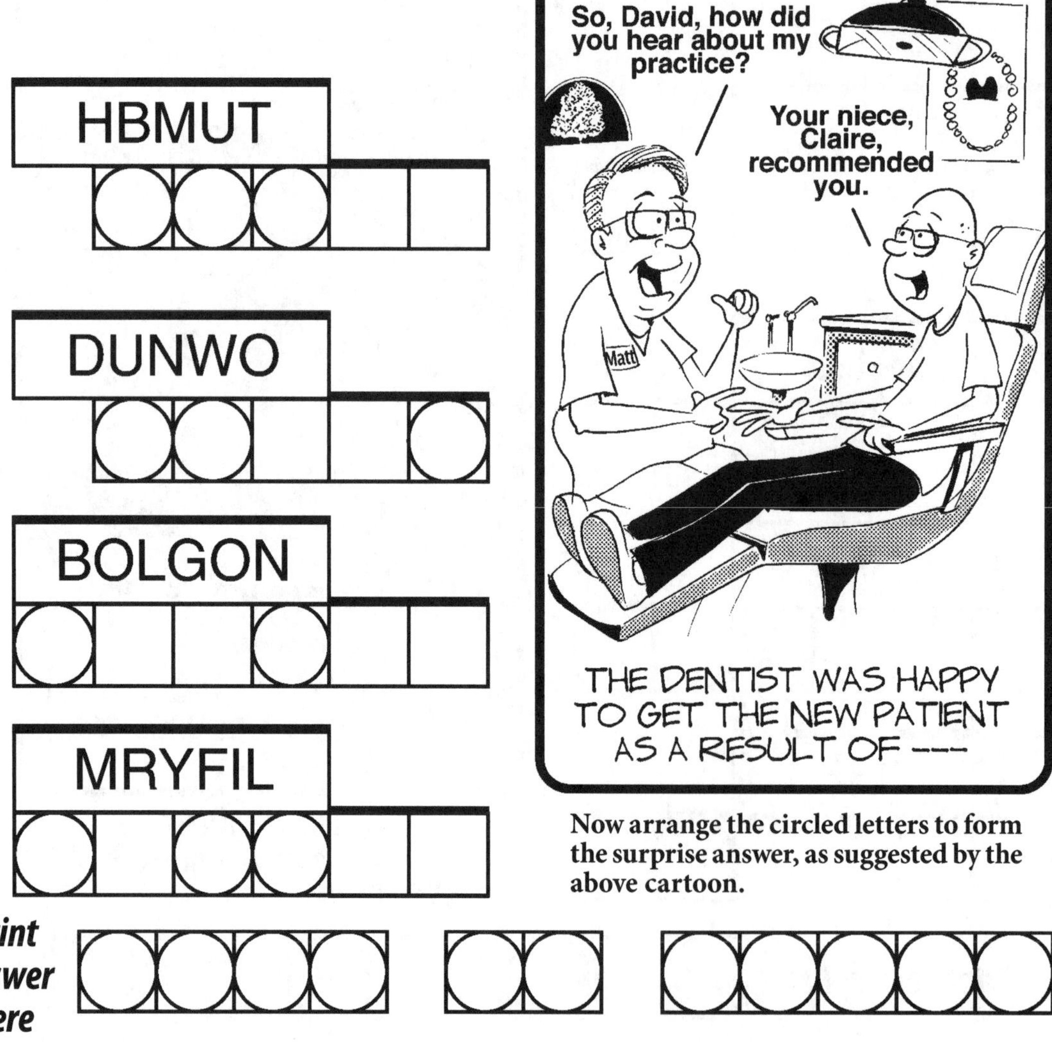
So, David, how did you hear about my practice?
Your niece, Claire, recommended you.
Matt
THE DENTIST WAS HAPPY TO GET THE NEW PATIENT AS A RESULT OF ---

Now arrange the circled letters to form the surprise answer, as suggested by the above cartoon.

Print answer here

PUZZLE
153

JUMBLE®

Unscramble these four Jumbles, one letter to each square, to form four ordinary words.

MURST
SIAAL
GINODI
IDONRO
As soon as we land, I'll head right out. Let's run through our checklist again.
You don't miss a thing!
WHEN IT CAME TO NEIL ARMSTRONG'S DETERMINATION TO WALK ON THE MOON, HE WAS ---

Now arrange the circled letters to form the surprise answer, as suggested by the above cartoon.

Print answer here

PUZZLE
154

JUMBLE®

Unscramble these four Jumbles, one letter to each square, to form four ordinary words.

VARAL

LATSL

FRUGIE

SUNEAA

King Family Reunion
It's OK. They've fought their whole lives.
Take him, son!
C'mon, boy. Teach your cousin a lesson.
No. He liked me better.
Grandpa liked me better!
THE FIGHT AT THE FAMILY REUNION WAS ---

Now arrange the circled letters to form the surprise answer, as suggested by the above cartoon.

Print answer here

PUZZLE
155

JUMBLE®

Unscramble these four Jumbles, one letter to each square, to form four ordinary words.

WARBN

TAYES

SOLENS

DRAIZL

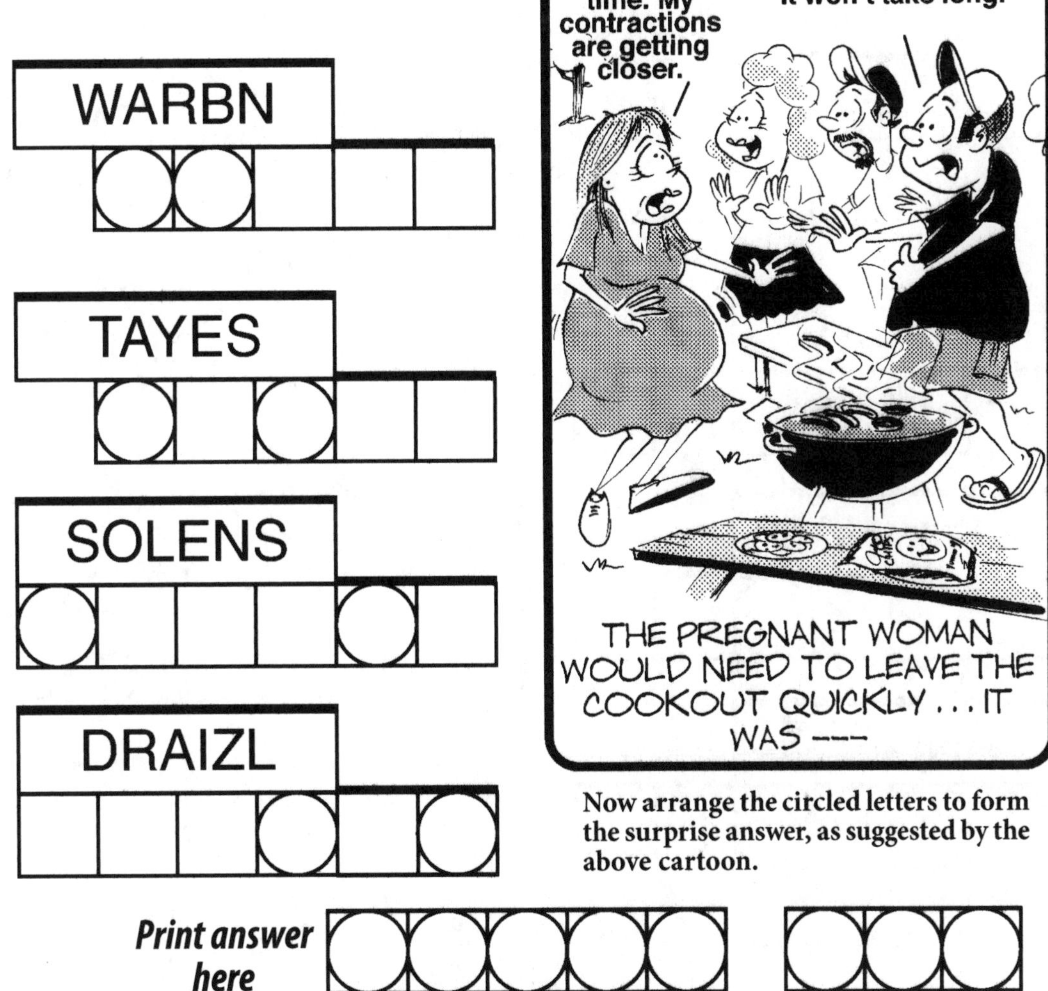
Honey, it's time. My contractions are getting closer.
I'll get the car. It won't take long.
THE PREGNANT WOMAN WOULD NEED TO LEAVE THE COOKOUT QUICKLY . . . IT WAS ---

Now arrange the circled letters to form the surprise answer, as suggested by the above cartoon.

Print answer here

PUZZLE
156

JUMBLE®

Unscramble these four Jumbles, one letter to each square, to form four ordinary words.

LIVAL
HOCAC
OYWHAN
ANNTET
No way.
Hey!
All finished!
That was fast. Too fast.
THE BIG CAT FINISHED THE TEST QUICKLY BECAUSE HE WAS A ---

Now arrange the circled letters to form the surprise answer, as suggested by the above cartoon.

Print answer here " - "

PUZZLE
157

JUMBLE®

Unscramble these four Jumbles, one letter to each square, to form four ordinary words.

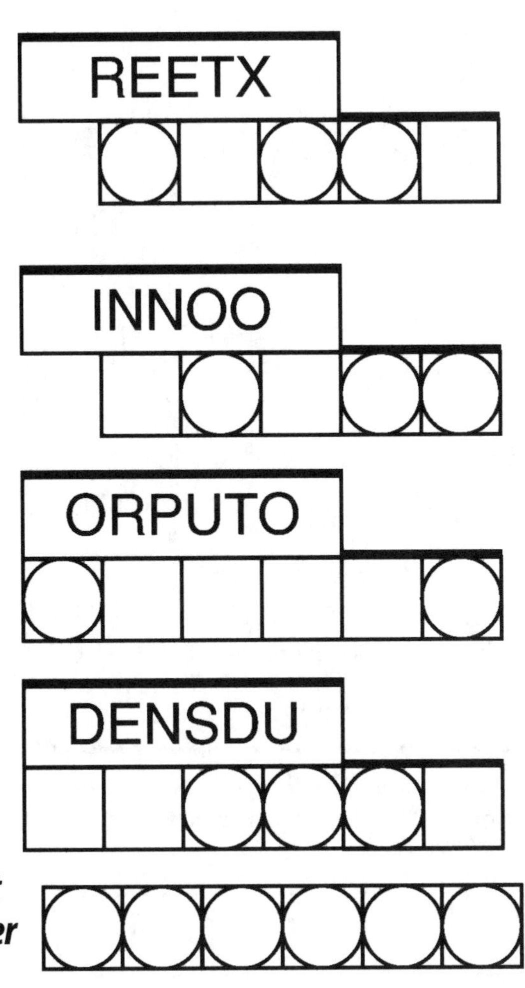
REETX
INNOO
ORPUTO
DENSDU

Great race!
Let's get something quick to eat.
Sorry. I have to dash.
FINISH
HE WANTED TO GO OUT TO LUNCH WITH HIS FRIENDS AFTER THE MARATHON, BUT HE ---

Now arrange the circled letters to form the surprise answer, as suggested by the above cartoon.

Print answer here

PUZZLE
158

JUMBLE®

Unscramble these four Jumbles, one letter to each square, to form four ordinary words.

DUELE

INJOT

CANYEG

SAYILE

Let's see what it is.
Looks like you got what you wanted.
Cool!
THE CYCLOPS' SON WANTED AN ACTION FIGURE FOR HIS BIRTHDAY, SO THEY BOUGHT HIM A ---

Now arrange the circled letters to form the surprise answer, as suggested by the above cartoon.

Print answer here ◯ - "◯◯◯" ◯◯◯

PUZZLE
159

JUMBLE®

Unscramble these four Jumbles, one letter to each square, to form four ordinary words.

RIHLW

CUEND

GLOREN

TRAMWH

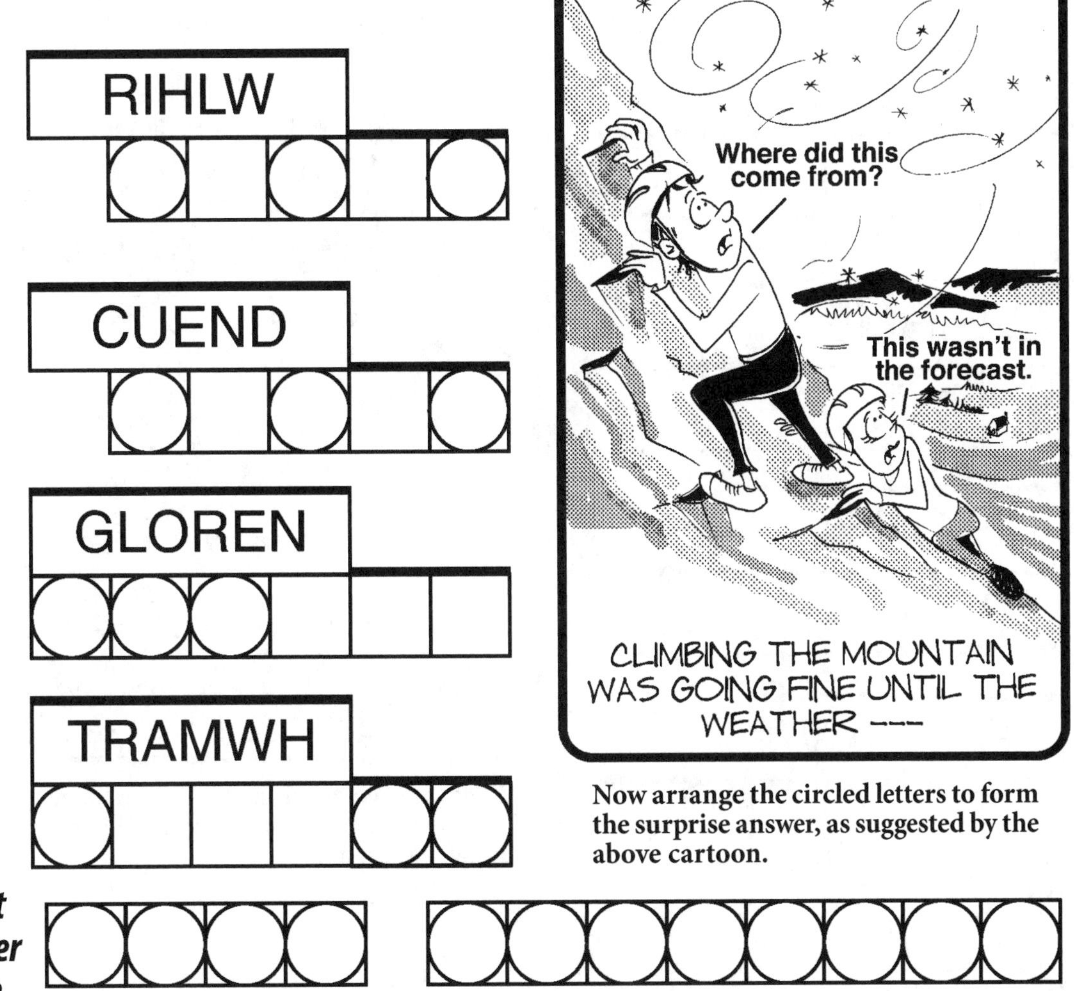
Where did this come from?
This wasn't in the forecast.
CLIMBING THE MOUNTAIN WAS GOING FINE UNTIL THE WEATHER ---

Now arrange the circled letters to form the surprise answer, as suggested by the above cartoon.

Print answer here

PUZZLE
160

JUMBLE®

Unscramble these four Jumbles, one letter to each square, to form four ordinary words.

SODTO

SIRMP

ICONEV

RELMAV

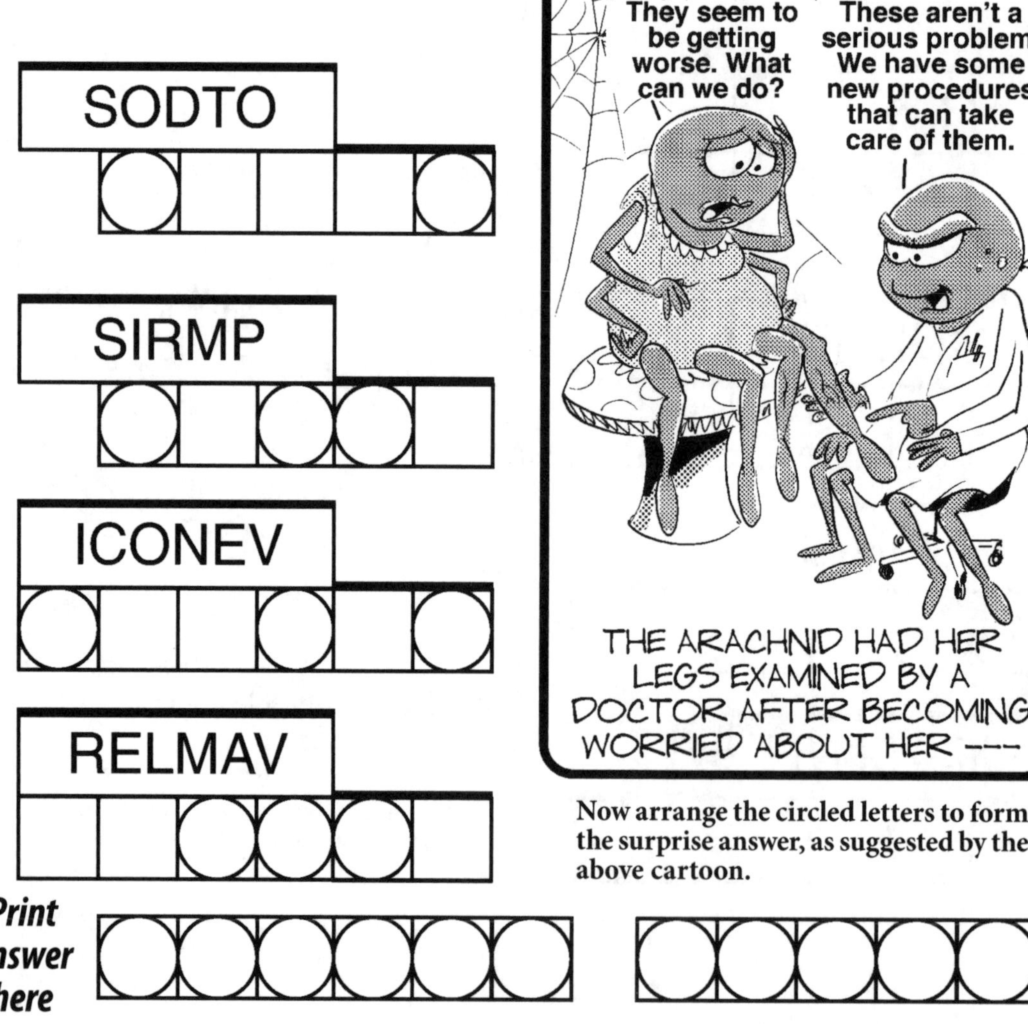
They seem to be getting worse. What can we do?
These aren't a serious problem. We have some new procedures that can take care of them.
THE ARACHNID HAD HER LEGS EXAMINED BY A DOCTOR AFTER BECOMING WORRIED ABOUT HER ---

Now arrange the circled letters to form the surprise answer, as suggested by the above cartoon.

Print answer here

JUMBLE®
Parachute

Challenger Puzzles

PUZZLE
161

JUMBLE®

Unscramble these six Jumbles, one letter to each square, to form six ordinary words.

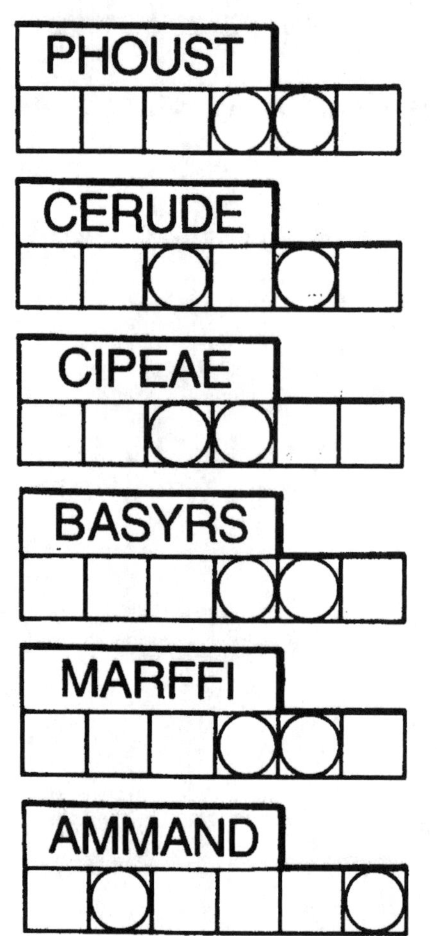
PHOUST
CERUDE
CIPEAE
BASYRS
MARFFI
AMMAND

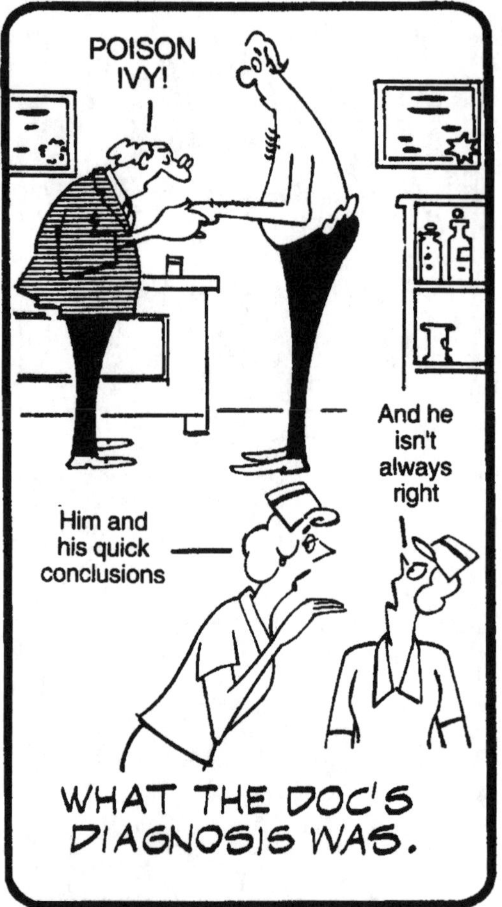
POISON IVY!
And he isn't always right
Him and his quick conclusions
WHAT THE DOC'S DIAGNOSIS WAS.

Now arrange the circled letters to form the surprise answer, as suggested by the above cartoon.

Print answer here

A " "

PUZZLE
162

JUMBLE®

Unscramble these six Jumbles, one letter to each square, to form six ordinary words.

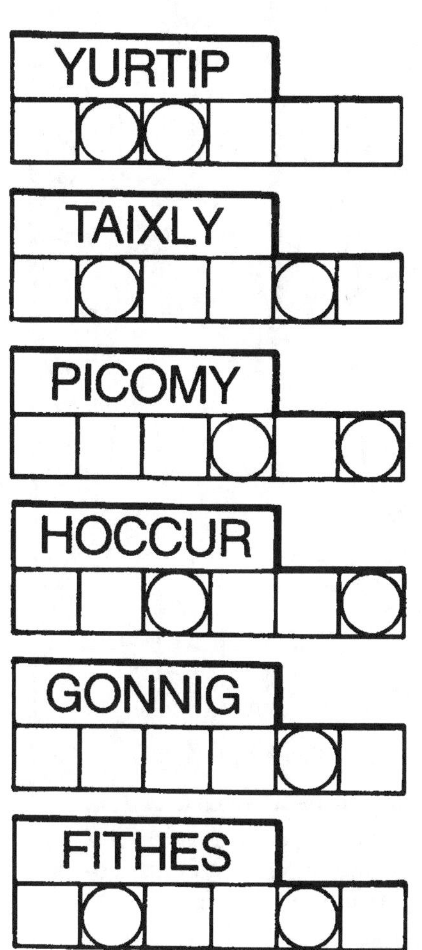
YURTIP
TAIXLY
PICOMY
HOCCUR
GONNIG
FITHES

If it doesn't open, pull the cord
WHAT THE SKYDIVERS USED.

Now arrange the circled letters to form the surprise answer, as suggested by the above cartoon.

Print answer here

A

JUMBLE®

Unscramble these six Jumbles, one letter to each square, to form six ordinary words.

STEGAK

POEQUA

WUCREF

DILBER

NUHLOY

YOSSIF

WHAT THE LATE-NIGHT DRUMMER FACED FROM HIS NEIGHBORS.

Now arrange the circled letters to form the surprise answer, as suggested by the above cartoon.

Print answer here

" ◯◯-◯◯◯◯◯◯◯◯◯◯◯ "

PUZZLE
164

JUMBLE®

Unscramble these six Jumbles, one letter to each square, to form six ordinary words.

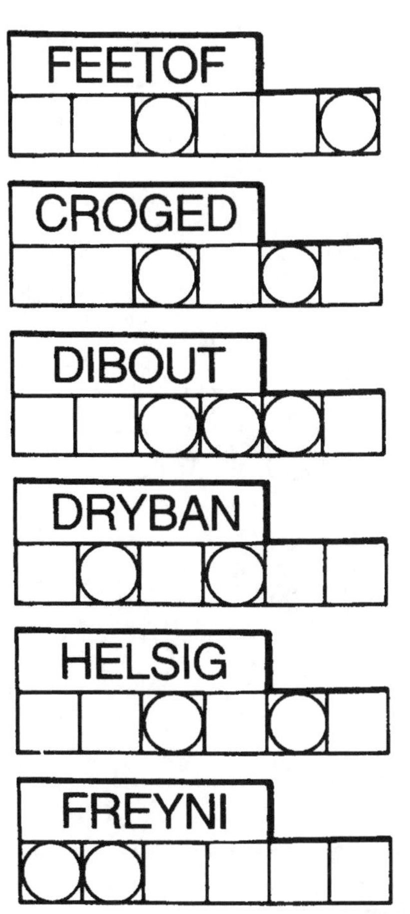
FEETOF
CROGED
DIBOUT
DRYBAN
HELSIG
FREYNI

Feel free to store your lunch here
WHAT THE WORKERS CONSIDERED THEIR USE OF THE COMPANY KITCHEN.

Now arrange the circled letters to form the surprise answer, as suggested by the above cartoon.

Print answer here

A " "

PUZZLE
165

JUMBLE®

Unscramble these six Jumbles, one letter to each square, to form six ordinary words.

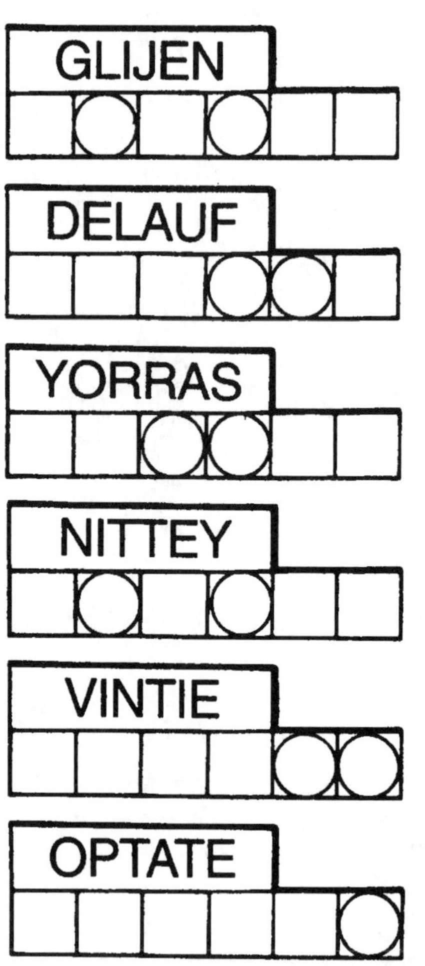
GLIJEN
DELAUF
YORRAS
NITTEY
VINTIE
OPTATE

I REFUSE TO WEAR 'EM
There's always one

Now arrange the circled letters to form the surprise answer, as suggested by the above cartoon.

Print answer here

THE

PUZZLE
166

JUMBLE®

Unscramble these six Jumbles, one letter to each square, to form six ordinary words.

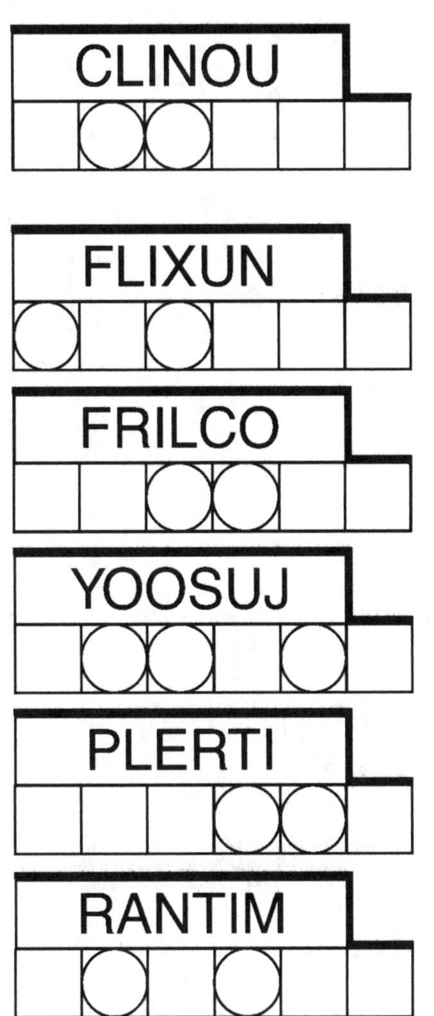
CLINOU
FLIXUN
FRILCO
YOOSUJ
PLERTI
RANTIM

BELIEVE
I want full coverage, no matter what happens
WHAT THE HOMEOWNER SOUGHT WHEN HE BOUGHT EARTHQUAKE INSURANCE.

Now arrange the circled letters to form the surprise answer, as suggested by the above cartoon.

Print answer here

A - “ ”

PUZZLE
167

JUMBLE®

Unscramble these six Jumbles, one letter to each square, to form six ordinary words.

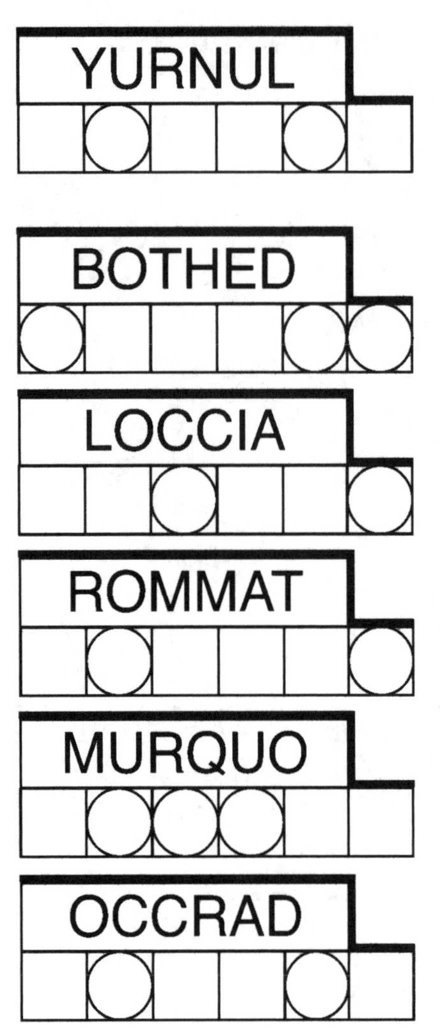
YURNUL
BOTHED
LOCCIA
ROMMAT
MURQUO
OCCRAD

I'm so sorry
Awful
You expect me to eat this?
WHAT THE DINERS GOT WHEN THEIR MEALS ARRIVED COLD.

Now arrange the circled letters to form the surprise answer, as suggested by the above cartoon.

Print answer here

THE

PUZZLE
168

JUMBLE®

Unscramble these six Jumbles, one letter to each square, to form six ordinary words.

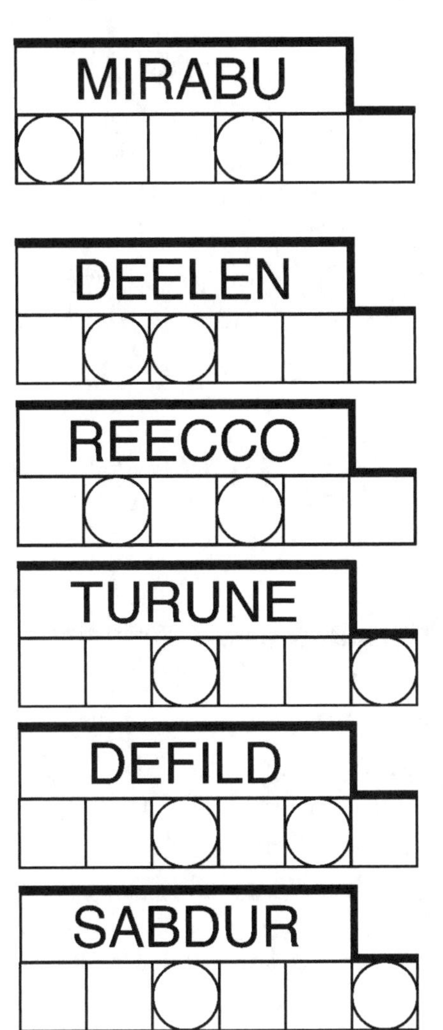
MIRABU
DEELEN
REECCO
TURUNE
DEFILD
SABDUR

I hope he left me something
He had millions, but who knows
WHAT THE ECCENTRIC TYCOON LEFT IN HIS WILL.

Now arrange the circled letters to form the surprise answer, as suggested by the above cartoon.

Print answer here

A
TO
“ ”

PUZZLE
169

JUMBLE®

Unscramble these six Jumbles, one letter to each square, to form six ordinary words.

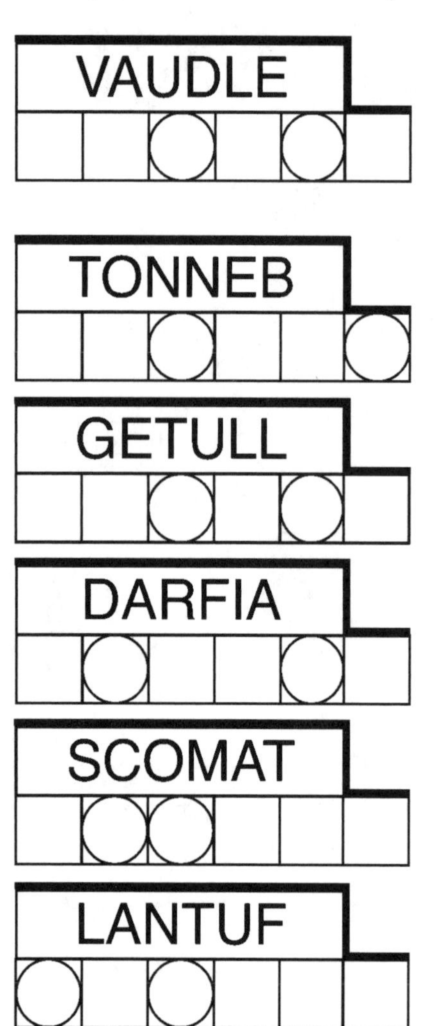
VAUDLE
TONNEB
GETULL
DARFIA
SCOMAT
LANTUF

Omigosh, I'm going 120
JUMBLE
JUMBLE
1
WHAT THE UPTIGHT LIBRARIAN EXPERIENCED WHEN SHE DROVE A RACE CAR.

Now arrange the circled letters to form the surprise answer, as suggested by the above cartoon.

Print answer here

IN THE

PUZZLE
170

JUMBLE®

Unscramble these six Jumbles, one letter to each square, to form six ordinary words.

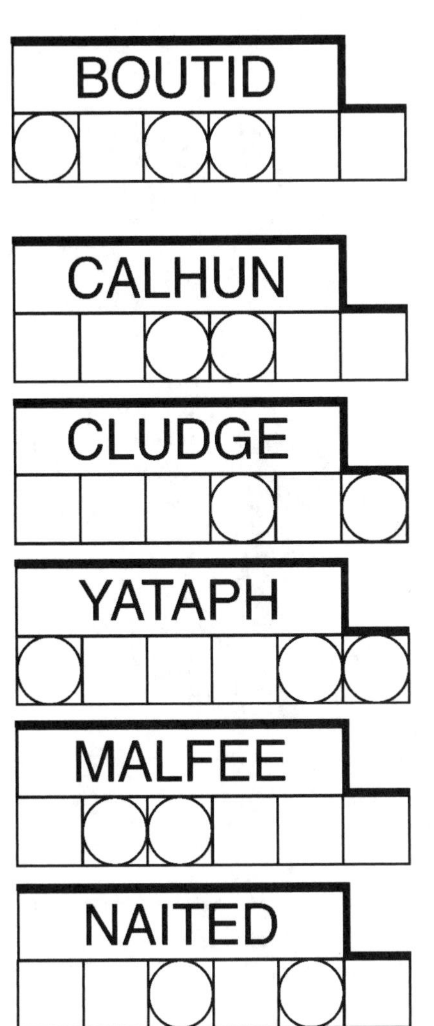
BOUTID
CALHUN
CLUDGE
YATAPH
MALFEE
NAITED

Oh, yeah? Where are they?
They were jumping into the boat
AN ANGLER EITHER HAS FISH LYING ABOUT HIM, OR HE'S ---

Now arrange the circled letters to form the surprise answer, as suggested by the above cartoon.

Print answer here

PUZZLE
171

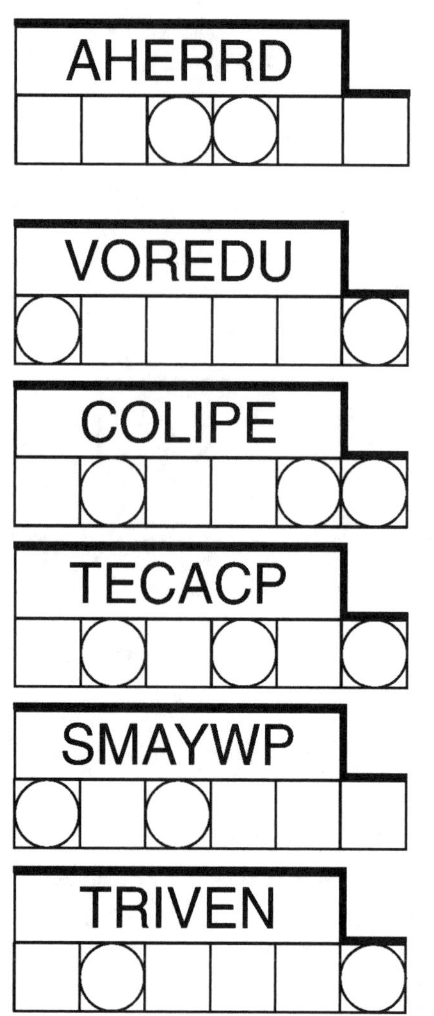
JUMBLE®
Unscramble these six Jumbles, one letter to each square, to form six ordinary words.
AHERRD
VOREDU
COLIPE
TECACP
SMAYWP
TRIVEN

JUMBLE
THE MOVIE
See! I told you so.
BEING THERE
You were right. I was wrong.
HE TOLD HIS WIFE THERE WOULDN'T BE A LINE TO SEE THE MOVIE, BUT HE WOULD ---

Now arrange the circled letters to form the surprise answer, as suggested by the above cartoon.

Print answer here

PUZZLE
172

JUMBLE®

Unscramble these six Jumbles, one letter to each square, to form six ordinary words.

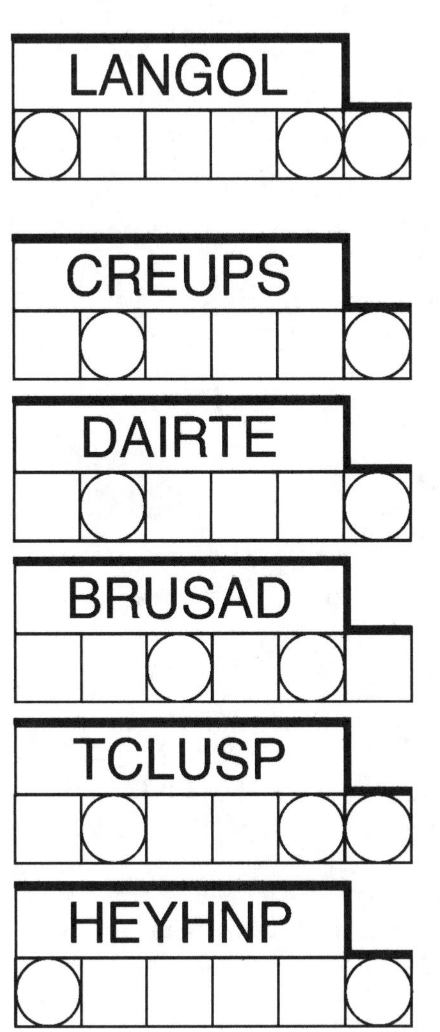
LANGOL
CREUPS
DAIRTE
BRUSAD
TCLUSP
HEYHNP

JUST JUMBLE
Mind the GAP
Leftorium
I love Black Friday.
Where to next?
Where are you?
THE MIDDLE OF THE MALL WAS THE ---

Now arrange the circled letters to form the surprise answer, as suggested by the above cartoon.

Print answer here

PUZZLE
173

JUMBLE®

Unscramble these six Jumbles, one letter to each square, to form six ordinary words.

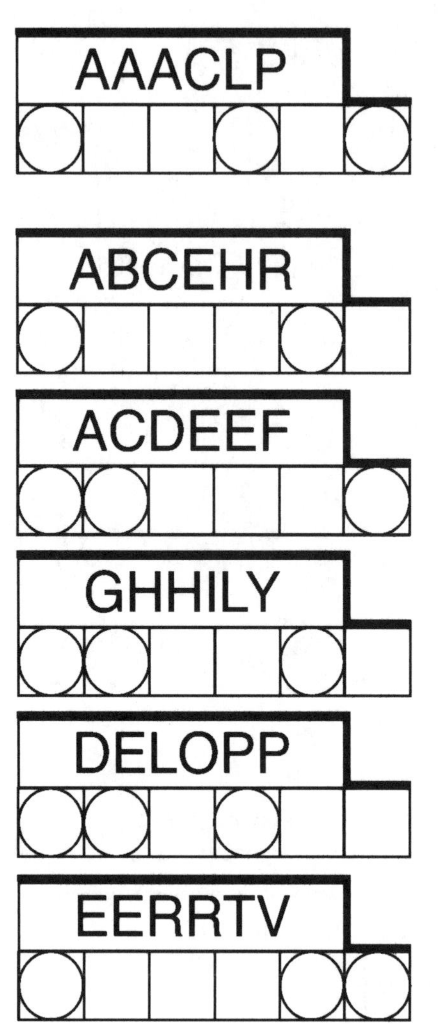
AAACLP
ABCEHR
ACDEEF
GHHILY
DELOPP
EERRTV

Where should I start?
Let's see. A: restock B: chase C: update Also, D: ...
A-G
H-P
Q-Z
WHEN THE LIBRARIAN GAVE HER NEW EMPLOYEE INSTRUCTIONS, SHE GAVE HER AN ---

Now arrange the circled letters to form the surprise answer, as suggested by the above cartoon.

Print answer here

PUZZLE
174

JUMBLE®

Unscramble these six Jumbles, one letter to each square, to form six ordinary words.

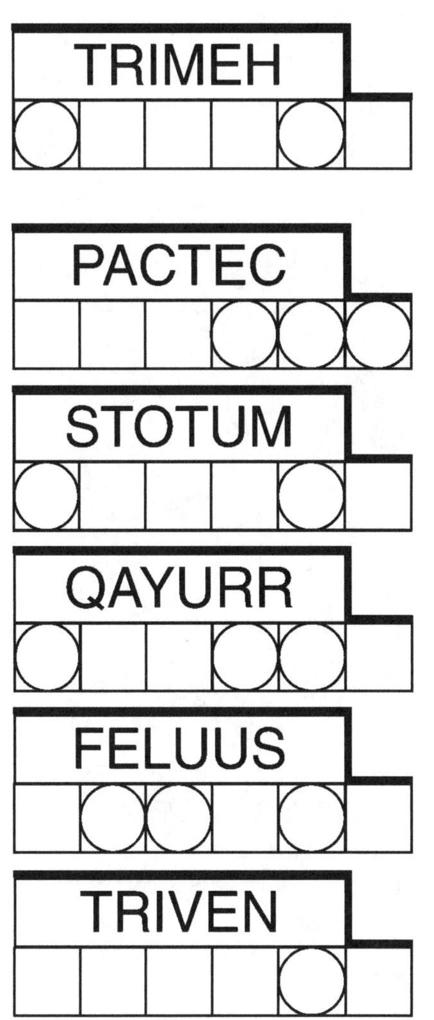
TRIMEH
PACTEC
STOTUM
QAYURR
FELUUS
TRIVEN

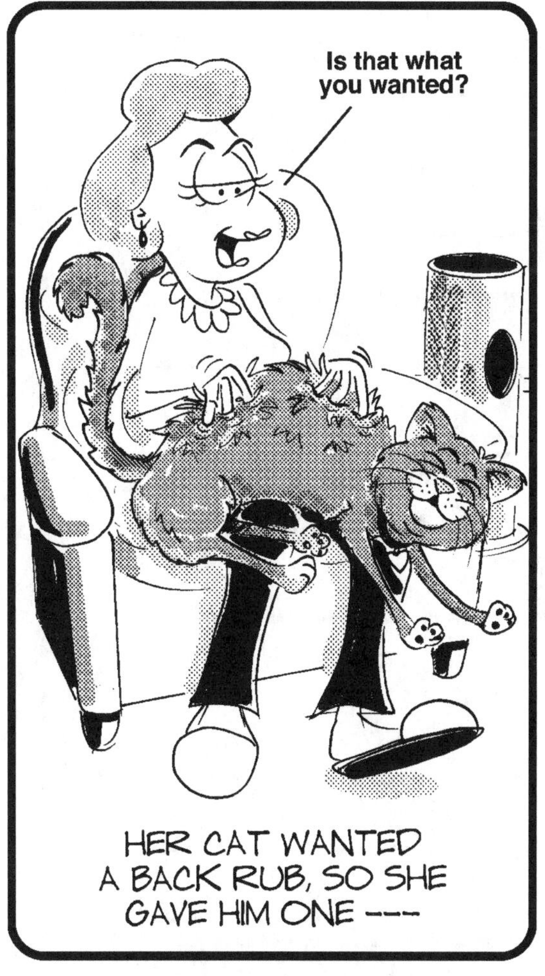
Is that what you wanted?
HER CAT WANTED A BACK RUB, SO SHE GAVE HIM ONE ---

Now arrange the circled letters to form the surprise answer, as suggested by the above cartoon.

Print answer here

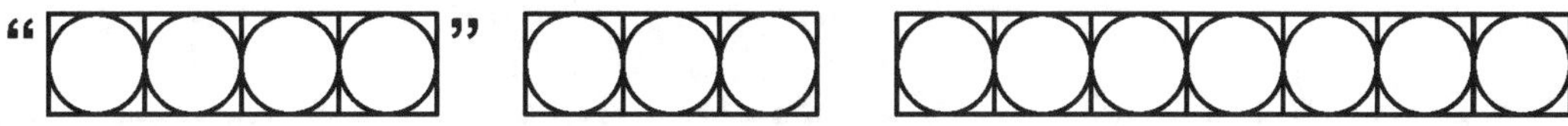

PUZZLE
175

JUMBLE®

Unscramble these six Jumbles, one letter to each square, to form six ordinary words.

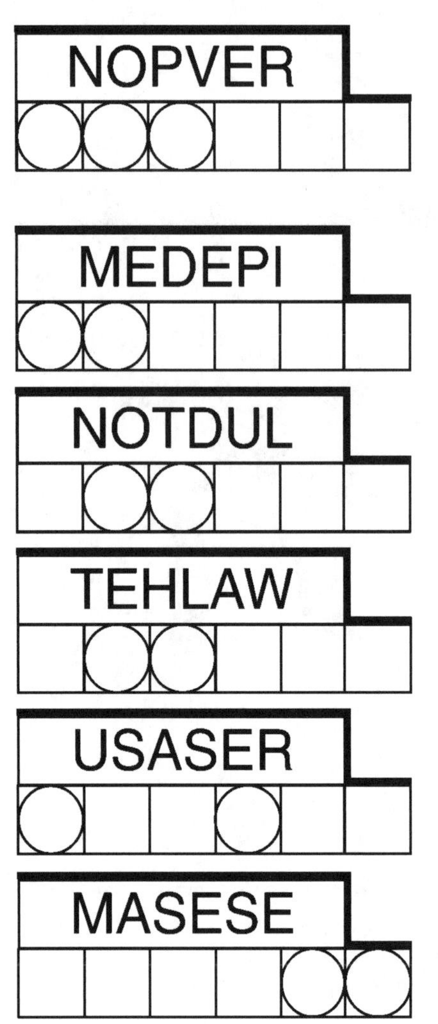
NOPVER
MEDEPI
NOTDUL
TEHLAW
USASER
MASESE

You can see, we have a lot of room for expansion.
U.S. FORD DEALERS
It looks like you're becoming the "King of Cars."
WHEN HENRY FORD'S BUSINESS EXPANDED, IT CREATED THE ---

Now arrange the circled letters to form the surprise answer, as suggested by the above cartoon.

Print answer here

PUZZLE

176

JUMBLE®

Unscramble these six Jumbles, one letter to each square, to form six ordinary words.

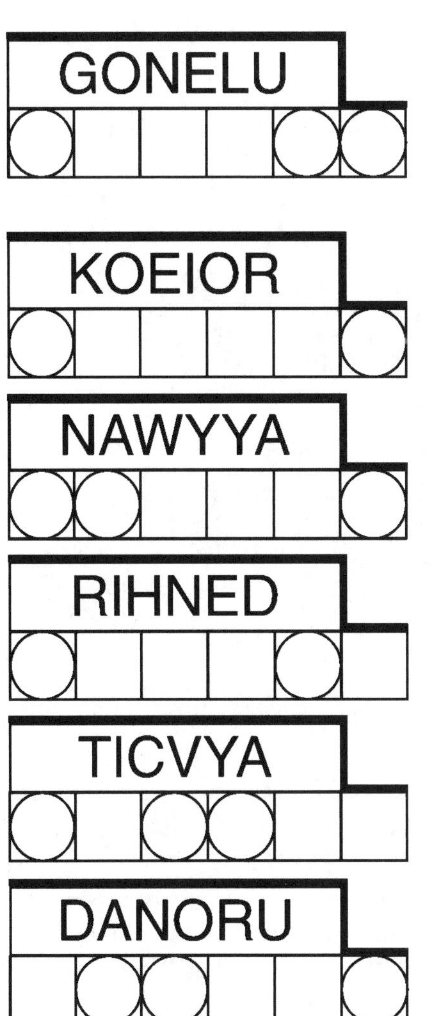
GONELU
KOEIOR
NAWYYA
RIHNED
TICVYA
DANORU

You're lucky the driver knew what he was doing.
How can I ever repay you?
You don't owe me anything. It was my honor to help you.
JUST JUMBLE MOBILE APP
AFTER THE WOMAN GAVE BIRTH IN THE TAXI, THE DRIVER TOLD HER THERE WAS ----

Now arrange the circled letters to form the surprise answer, as suggested by the above cartoon.

Print answer here

PUZZLE
177

JUMBLE®

Unscramble these six Jumbles, one letter to each square, to form six ordinary words.

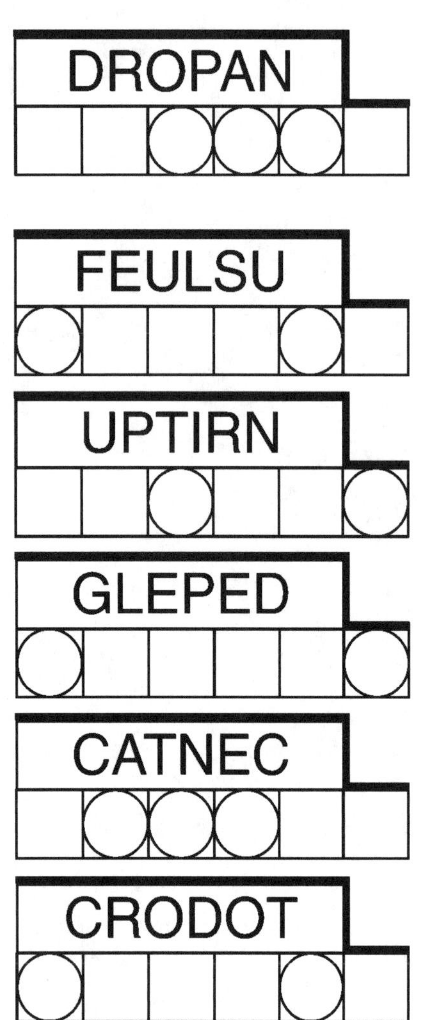
DROPAN
FEULSU
UPTIRN
GLEPED
CATNEC
CRODOT

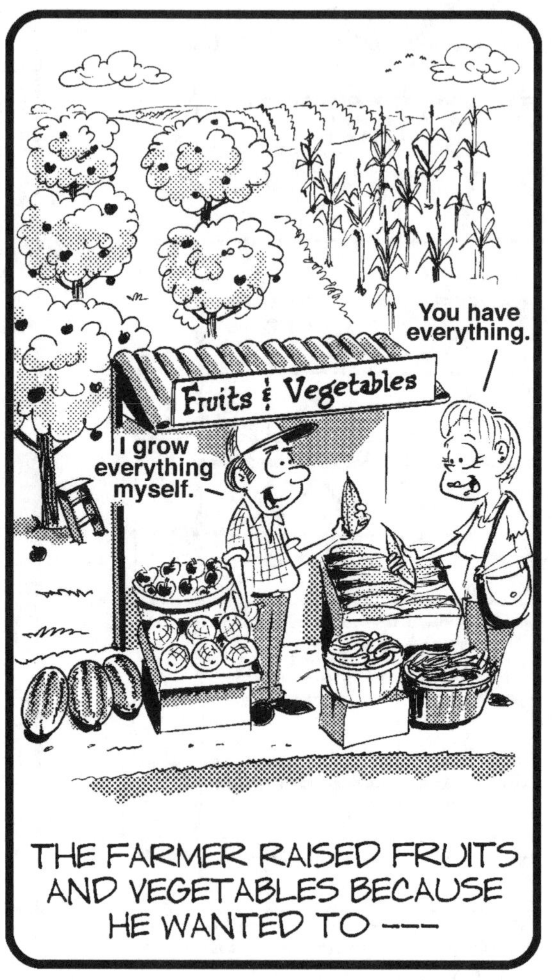
Fruits & Vegetables
You have everything.
I grow everything myself.
THE FARMER RAISED FRUITS AND VEGETABLES BECAUSE HE WANTED TO ---

Now arrange the circled letters to form the surprise answer, as suggested by the above cartoon.

Print answer here

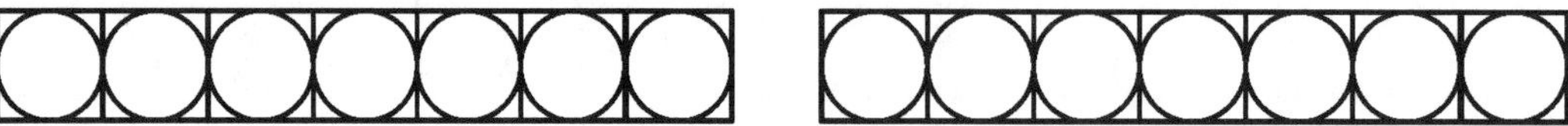

PUZZLE
178

JUMBLE®

Unscramble these six Jumbles, one letter to each square, to form six ordinary words.

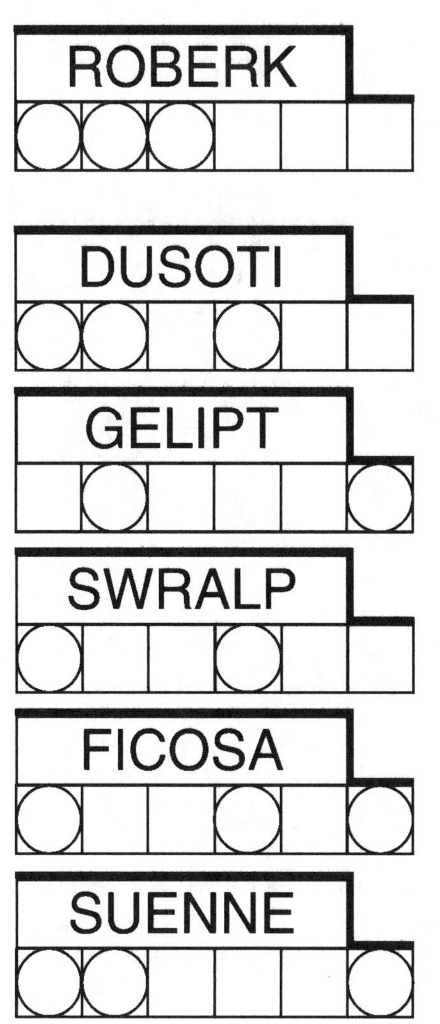
ROBERK
DUSOTI
GELIPT
SWRALP
FICOSA
SUENNE

Are you really going to quit this time? No excuses?
Yes! This is it. I'm doing it for sure.
THIS TIME HE WAS REALLY GOING TO QUIT SMOKING, ---

Now arrange the circled letters to form the surprise answer, as suggested by the above cartoon.

Print answer here

PUZZLE
179

JUMBLE®

Unscramble these six Jumbles, one letter to each square, to form six ordinary words.

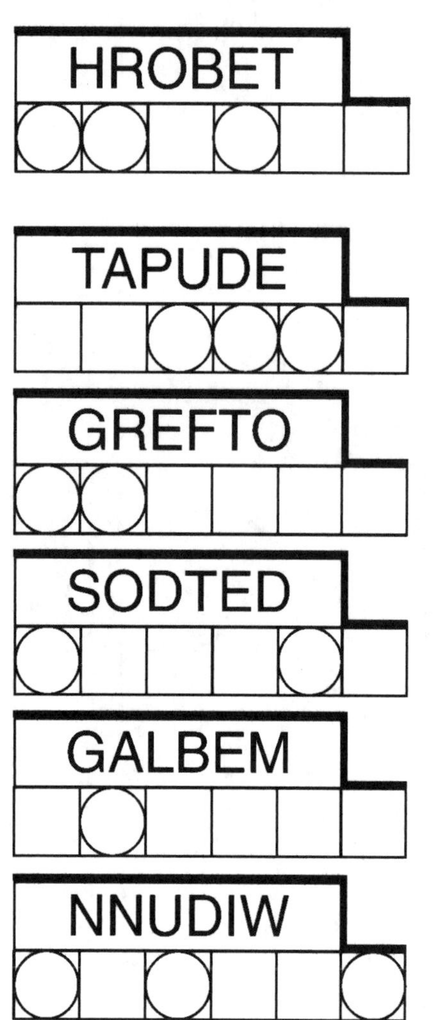
HROBET
TAPUDE
GREFTO
SODTED
GALBEM
NNUDIW

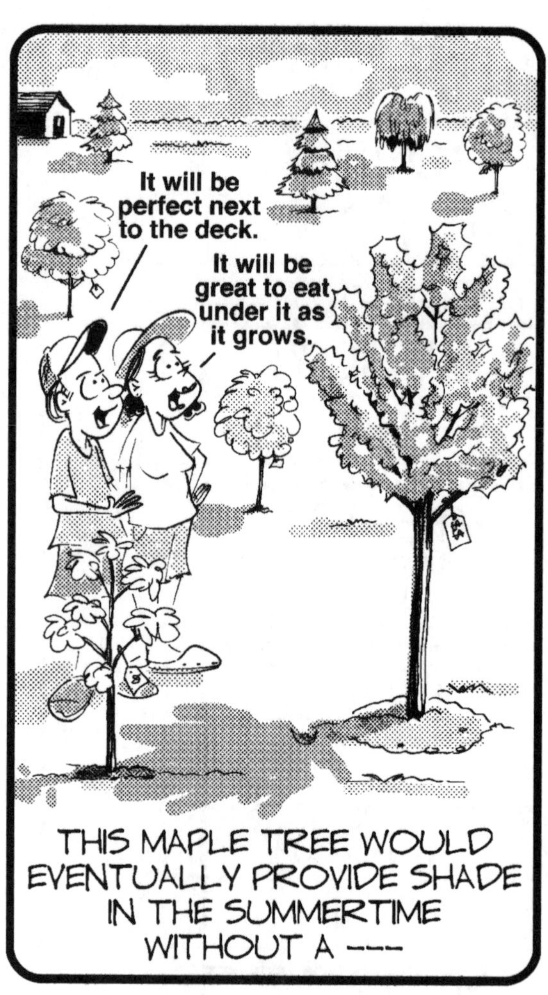
It will be perfect next to the deck.
It will be great to eat under it as it grows.
THIS MAPLE TREE WOULD EVENTUALLY PROVIDE SHADE IN THE SUMMERTIME WITHOUT A ---

Now arrange the circled letters to form the surprise answer, as suggested by the above cartoon.

Print answer here

PUZZLE
180

JUMBLE®

Unscramble these six Jumbles, one letter to each square, to form six ordinary words.

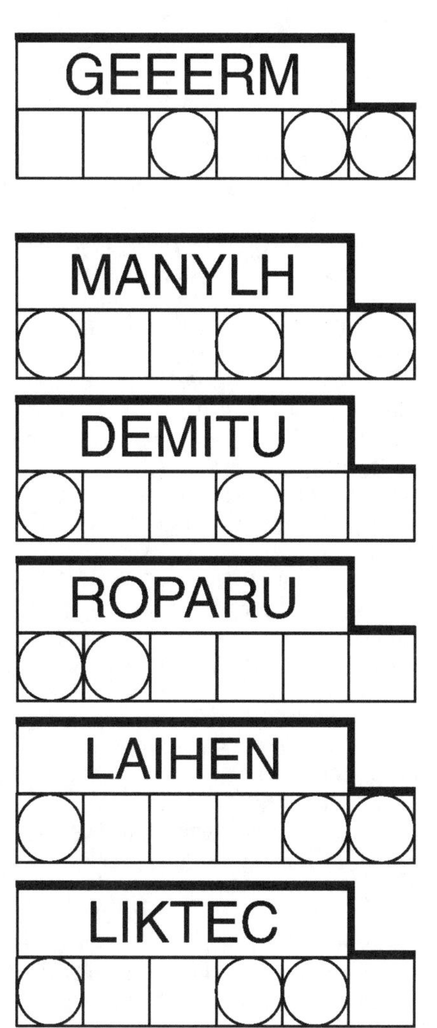
GEEERM
MANYLH
DEMITU
ROPARU
LAIHEN
LIKTEC

Dr. Orin Scrivello, D.D.S.
Nooo! I don't have any cavities!
Why are you being so difficult?
GETTING HER SON TO THE DENTIST WAS ---

Now arrange the circled letters to form the surprise answer, as suggested by the above cartoon.

Print answer here

Answers

1. **Jumbles:** BARON ELATE PATTER INFORM
Answer: One way to be a fool—FOOL WITH A BEE
2. **Jumbles:** PANIC WHOSE QUAINT SKEWER
Answer: How to find out a tightrope walker's secret—TAP HIS WIRE
3. **Jumbles:** UTTER AROMA HANGAR GLOBAL
Answer: What the guys who stole the sheep were—ON THE "LAMB"
4. **Jumbles:** TASTY KHAKI DISMAL FARINA
Answer: What they called the paramedics' mascot—THE FIRST-AID "KIT"
5. **Jumbles:** NOOSE PARTY STANZA FINISH
Answer: The point about this is that it's kept hidden—A SAFETY PIN
6. **Jumbles:** NEWSY DUNCE EMBODY OUTING
Answer: If the bride looked stunning, how did the groom look?—STUNNED
7. **Jumbles:** VERVE HIKER INNATE ATOMIC
Answer: They might be shown with a smile—TEETH
8. **Jumbles:** MOUSY HOARD PACKET QUARRY
Answer: A trick that takes us in—A "R-US-E"
9. **Jumbles:** POWER TYING FERVOR HAPPEN
Answer: By the time a man is wise enough to watch his step, he's usually too old to do this—GO ANYWHERE
10. **Jumbles:** GASSY BERTH NESTLE DEFACE
Answer: A soft touch—A CARESS
11. **Jumbles:** GAWKY IRONY TUSSLE DAINTY
Answer: The sailor turned minister was skilled at this—TYING KNOTS
12. **Jumbles:** VAPOR ELITE THORAX CIPHER
Answer: Is it going to be a local or a general anesthetic?—"YOU CAN HAVE ETHER"
13. **Jumbles:** VENOM BRIAR OUTING HALLOW
Answer: The miner didn't know whether he had struck this—IRON ORE WHAT
14. **Jumbles:** UTTER JUICE DURESS ADJOIN
Answer: What the lawyer demanded to have with his drink—"JUST ICE"
15. **Jumbles:** TEMPO UNCLE KOWTOW SHANTY
Answer: Who's heard about the big kidnapping?—"HE WOKE UP"
16. **Jumbles:** FAIRY ENEMY PAUPER TALLOW
Answer: What the ram said to the female of the species—I'M AFTER EWE
17. **Jumbles:** LYRIC BULLY FORMAL PILFER
Answer: How she slipped into her bikini—"BRIEF-LY"
18. **Jumbles:** SKUNK EPOCH OBTUSE MISHAP
Answer: What the new father of quintuplets just couldn't believe—HIS "CENSUS"
19. **Jumbles:** CEASE ALTAR BELLOW DEFACE
Answer: The crooked architect discovered that prison walls weren't built this way—TO SCALE
20. **Jumbles:** SNORT ALIAS SAILOR EXPOSE
Answer: It was his last meal, but you should have seen this—HOW THE ASSASSINATE (assassin ate)
21. **Jumbles:** TWINE FAITH BISHOP PLURAL
Answer: The librarian also cried when she saw her books were this—IN "TIERS"
22. **Jumbles:** ELEGY DECRY WISELY SCORCH
Answer: What the finicky dog was—"CHEW-SY"
23. **Jumbles:** CUBIT AWASH FLATLY DECENT
Answer: What you might get if you stand too close to an irritated donkey—A SEAT "BELT"
24. **Jumbles:** LIBEL CANAL BEHOLD DAWNED
Answer: What the rabbits who were playing in the onion patch had—A "BAWL"
25. **Jumbles:** FEINT BATCH AGENDA BEWAIL
Answer: He was always going around in circles because he thought he was this—A BIG WHEEL
26. **Jumbles:** PIVOT HONOR MISUSE BIKINI
Answer: What the gambling addict had trouble balancing—HIS BOOKIES
27. **Jumbles:** ADAGE VILLA CYMBAL JARGON
Answer: A hypocrite is someone who can't tell the truth without doing this—LYING
28. **Jumbles:** KETCH VISTA EYELET FUNGUS
Answer: Can you get fur from a skunk?—"IF YOU'RE LUCKY"
29. **Jumbles:** DITTY AFOOT BUBBLE TACKLE
Answer: What a girl who wants to be married has to know how to do—TIE A "BEAU"
30. **Jumbles:** DALLY BEFIT RECTOR HELIUM
Answer: What she called that sour husband of hers—HER "BITTER" HALF
31. **Jumbles:** MIDGE GUMBO BUZZER NORMAL
Answer: What the coach did every time a player fumbled—MUMBLED
32. **Jumbles:** SWASH BURST VIABLE COUPLE
Answer: What a beauty contest judge has to know how to do—PASS ON CURVES
33. **Jumbles:** NERVY CHAFF ZIGZAG ENCORE
Answer: What you might do if you try to paint a girl in the nude—FREEZE
34. **Jumbles:** HURRY ANISE INTENT DOMINO
Answer: She couldn't cook worth a darn, but she sure knew how to do this—DISH IT OUT
35. **Jumbles:** GAMUT PROXY FUSION DEBTOR
Answer: They decided to appoint him chief cook because he had this—THE "POT" FOR IT
36. **Jumbles:** SHAKY BLOAT NATURE IMPEDE
Answer: Samson loved Delilah until she did this—"BALD" HIM OUT
37. **Jumbles:** VITAL MUSIC NINETY FICKLE
Answer: Why he insisted on wearing seat belts—TO SAVE HIS KIN
38. **Jumbles:** CROUP LARVA HARROW BELONG
Answer: How many pounds of limburger cheese do you want?—A "PHEW"
39. **Jumbles:** NOBLE SHEAF GIGGLE INFECT
Answer: What that frustrated astronaut was always doing at home—BLASTING OFF
40. **Jumbles:** CASTE BRAND GUTTER ABDUCT
Answer: Although man does not live by bread alone, he may get by on this—"CRUST"
41. **Jumbles:** FORGO COVEY PYTHON ALKALI
Answer: What the "love affair" she was carrying on with all those soldiers must have been—"PLATOON-IC"
42. **Jumbles:** RURAL BANAL UNWISE IMPORT
Answer: A feeling you get when you open your mail on the first of the month—"BILL-IOUS"
43. **Jumbles:** VERVE BELLE TRAGIC AIRWAY
Answer: What they called the man who put glass into the igloo windows—THE "GLACIER"
44. **Jumbles:** EAGLE GASSY KITTEN MYSTIC
Answer: What that long tour made him—"SEE" SICK

45. **Jumbles:** SAVOR WRATH FELLOW EXEMPT
Answer: What his neighbor said when he showed off his new lawn equipment—"MOWER" POWER TO YOU

46. **Jumbles:** TOXIN MINUS HANGAR FIRING
Answer: What those boxers engaged in while having a few drinks—"INN" FIGHTING

47. **Jumbles:** DOUBT FOAMY EVOLVE NUDISM
Answer: When she asked for a diamond, he turned this—"STONE" DEAF

48. **Jumbles:** BROIL RAJAH LIKELY POSTAL
Answer: Orthopedic surgeons must be lucky when they get this—ALL THE BREAKS

49. **Jumbles:** APPLY CHAIR DIVERT HUNGRY
Answer: What kind of youngster does basketball usually attract?—A VERY HIGH TYPE

50. **Jumbles:** FAIRY ELITE POWDER LAUNCH
Answer: What they called that crooked politician turned doctor—THE WARD "HEALER"

51. **Jumbles:** DITTO WHEAT TRICKY HALLOW
Answer: How children arrive at your door tonight—EVERY "WITCH" WAY

52. **Jumbles:** BASIC COCOA CALIPH FRIEZE
Answer: It's "said" to be a test—"ORAL"

53. **Jumbles:** LEAKY ERASE INVITE FACILE
Answer: What too much of an open mind might be like—A SIEVE

54. **Jumbles:** PIPER EXILE MAKEUP TAMPER
Answer: Another name for a pawnbroker—A "TIME KEEPER"

55. **Jumbles:** ERUPT FLOOR DELUXE GEYSER
Answer: At the seashore, your composure is often distracted by this—EXPOSURE

56. **Jumbles:** PATCH CIVIL HICCUP TAUGHT
Answer: What a marriage proposal is—A HITCH PITCH

57. **Jumbles:** MAIZE GOING TUXEDO PENCIL
Answer: The only reason they called him a big shot was that he was always doing this—EXPLODING

58. **Jumbles:** BLOOD POKER NAUGHT SMUDGE
Answer: What that good-looking dog was—"HOUNDSOME"

59. **Jumbles:** PILOT MAGIC SPRUCE CENSUS
Answer: You'd get no praises from this—AN "ASPERSION"

60. **Jumbles:** ENTRY IMPEL CHALET BALSAM
Answer: Where armaments might be found naturally—AMONG "MEN-AT-ARMS"

61. **Jumbles:** ROBIN LIMIT MARTIN ABOUND
Answer: What she called her husband who was an amateur ornithologist—"BIRD BRAIN"

62. **Jumbles:** BATON AGILE ENJOIN HITHER
Answer: What to do in order to have soft white hands—NOTHING

63. **Jumbles:** DELVE EVENT SNAPPY OSSIFY
Answer: What the nervous disc jockey lives on—SPINS & NEEDLES

64. **Jumbles:** FORUM GAUZE EXTANT DULCET
Answer: The reason so many of us are discontented with our lot these days is that it's no longer this—A LOT

65. **Jumbles:** NEEDY PERKY SIMILE RATION
Answer: What life was for the guy who spent all his time at that "singles" spot—JUST "MEET" & DRINK

66. **Jumbles:** MOUTH APART LADING NETHER
Answer: What a woman might attempt to draw with an eyebrow pencil—ATTENTION

67. **Jumbles:** NOISY DOILY PASTRY NUDISM
Answer: This may determine what kind of position you have in life—YOUR DISPOSITION

68. **Jumbles:** BANDY TEMPO DULCET CHEERY
Answer: What the "ham" was for the drama critic—HIS "MEAT"

69. **Jumbles:** NIECE CROUP EXPOSE VANISH
Answer: He called her "dear" before marriage and afterwards this—"EXPENSIVE"

70. **Jumbles:** PYLON FUDGE CASHEW DITHER
Answer: A girl who now tells him where to take her might later tell him this—WHERE TO GO

71. **Jumbles:** GOOSE WAGER VICUNA JOYFUL
Answer: That big talker's listeners got no chance to open their mouths except for this—YAWNS

72. **Jumbles:** KNELL TABOO PUZZLE MEMBER
Answer: What sailing a boat on a nice windy day can be—A BREEZE

73. **Jumbles:** VISOR DICED PARODY BICEPS
Answer: What she did when she discovered that her boyfriend was a crooked gambler—"DIS-CARDED" HIM

74. **Jumbles:** ELITE POKER SUBWAY KERNEL
Answer: Another name for a plagiarist—A "STEAL" WORKER

75. **Jumbles:** QUEEN BELLE BISHOP MAGPIE
Answer: A fisherman sometimes stands still while fishing, but more often does this—LIES

76. **Jumbles:** TAWNY WOVEN PARITY MORGUE
Answer: What an untalented writer might earn by his pen—"PEN-URY"

77. **Jumbles:** VISTA NATAL SCHOOL BETRAY
Answer: What her old flame turned out to be—A SILLY "ASH"

78. **Jumbles:** MAXIM PUTTY BELLOW GARLIC
Answer: How the scandal-monger let the cat out of the bag—ONE CLAW AT A TIME

79. **Jumbles:** DITTO ALIAS LAUNCH BURLAP
Answer: What kind of jokes do those mountain folk tell?—"HILL-ARIOUS" ONES

80. **Jumbles:** BAGGY AFTER FAMISH POUNCE
Answer: Wallpapering is easy once you get this—THE HANG OF IT

81. **Jumbles:** AHEAD VOCAL DECEIT GASKET
Answer: What the politician did when his opponent "laid an egg."—CACKLED

82. **Jumbles:** TONIC CHASM PARLOR RADIUS
Answer: The egotist found fault with everything except this—HIS MIRROR

83. **Jumbles:** ADULT HAVEN NEARLY EFFACE
Answer: What a good dancer has to be—"HANDY" WITH HIS FEET

84. **Jumbles:** NEWSY VITAL MARTYR CLEAVE
Answer: Some people are richer than others, which proves that wealth may be only this—"RELATIVE"

85. **Jumbles:** MOUNT QUOTA AUBURN CAUGHT
Answer: That offensive talker had a tongue so sharp he almost did this—CUT HIS OWN THROAT

86. **Jumbles:** EXILE RUSTY GYRATE CHARGE
Answer: What the spendthrift ended up making—HIS "HEIRS" TURN GRAY

87. **Jumbles:** BILGE ABOUT RARELY FIDDLE
Answer: What a man given to horselaughs should be—"BRIDLED"

88. **Jumbles:** RODEO LIVEN WORTHY EMBALM
Answer: He offered to help with the lawn because he needed this—"MOWER MONEY" (more money)

89. **Jumbles:** BIRCH SWASH PONDER MARVEL
Answer: A woman without a heart might make a fool of a man without this—A HEAD

90. **Jumbles:** PIETY ICILY TROLLY BAFFLE
Answer: His inability to tell the truth turned out to be this for him—A "LIE-ABILITY"

91. **Jumbles:** SWAMP CHICK PLURAL BURLAP
Answer: The door to success is usually open to people who have lots of this—PUSH & PULL

92. **Jumbles:** APRON FORCE CANOPY HECKLE
Answer: What that arrogant insect was—A COCKY ROACH

93. **Jumbles:** OPIUM FISHY SLOUCH NINETY
Answer: When he proposed that they get married, she told him that the outcome would depend on this—HIS INCOME

94. **Jumbles:** TAFFY HONEY EIGHTY CONCUR
Answer: You show poise when you raise your eyebrows instead of this—THE ROOF

95. **Jumbles:** GLEAM FORTY SULTRY PULPIT
Answer: If your "pancake" makeup isn't all you expected it to be, you might try adding this—MAPLE SYRUP

96. **Jumbles:** MINER NAVAL STRONG ORIOLE
Answer: The right time to buy a boat—WHEN THERE'S A "SAIL" ON IT

97. **Jumbles:** PARKA LIBEL BLEACH DEADLY
Answer: The fortune-teller said she liked her work because she always did this—"HAD A BALL"

98. **Jumbles:** WAGON CLOAK FLATLY RADIUS
Answer: That so-called financial advisor is always ready to back his judgment with this—YOUR LAST DOLLAR

99. **Jumbles:** FENCE DRAFT HOPPER THRESH
Answer: If someone is now celebrating his birthday, there's no gift like this—THE "PRESENT"

100. **Jumbles:** PIVOT DOWNY FAULTY BECOME
Answer: Where you might see a shooting star—IN A COWBOY FILM

101. **Jumbles:** BASIS FEIGN SCROLL THROAT
Answer: Love at first sight sometimes breaks up at—FIRST SLIGHT

102. **Jumbles:** DERBY GLADE RANCID CLUMSY
Answer: What he hoped this exercise would do to his body fat—RECYCLE IT

103. **Jumbles:** LEGAL HYENA VASSAL FEEBLE
Answer: Some fashions are cut to this—"SEE" LEVEL

104. **Jumbles:** SHEEP EXACT MARROW TAWDRY
Answer: If you lend a pretended "friend" money, and never see him again—IT WAS WORTH IT

105. **Jumbles:** RUSTY HAVEN AWEIGH FONDLY
Answer: What they said to the nut who claimed to have invented a new type of sieve—"THAT WON'T HOLD WATER"

106. **Jumbles:** PUTTY GROIN DEVICE MASCOT
Answer: The opportunist has no use for friends—HE CAN'T "USE"

107. **Jumbles:** BAKED AFOOT RADIUM VERMIN
Answer: What the sailor shouted when he saw the surfer—MAN "OVER BOARD"

108. **Jumbles:** ELITE HEFTY SNAPPY TORRID
Answer: At the end of that shopping spree, she was—TIRED AS WELL AS "SPENT"

109. **Jumbles:** UNIFY GLOAT DEFAME FROTHY
Answer: She decided to break up with the seismologist because, he was such a—"FAULT" FINDER

110. **Jumbles:** SHINY FOAMY UNFAIR COHORT
Answer: A rich relative is always close to you until you try to—"TOUCH" HIM

111. **Jumbles:** CARGO WHEEL BYWORD HAZARD
Answer: How the miser accumulated all that money—THE "HOARD" WAY

112. **Jumbles:** HOIST ANNUL YELLOW GHETTO
Answer: He found it difficult to stoop—TO ANYTHING LOW

113. **Jumbles:** TRUTH PRIZE EMBARK GULLET
Answer: He seemed to be sawing wood in his slumber because this was in it—"LUMBER"

114. **Jumbles:** CAPON RAPID NUDISM TIMELY
Answer: What the egotist was suffering from—"I" STRAIN

115. **Jumbles:** SHAKY HOARD MOTIVE JESTER
Answer: What the cute little potato was warned against—MASHERS

116. **Jumbles:** IRONY JOUST NOTIFY CURFEW
Answer: What the chiropractor and his wife were working on—A JOINT RETURN

117. **Jumbles:** MOSSY GROUP MORGUE EITHER—What boarding house gossip used to start with—"ROOMERS"

118. **Jumbles:** BASSO ARMOR TACKLE STUCCO
Answer: What the twelve bottles of moonshine eventually became—A COURT CASE

119. **Jumbles:** TASTY PRIME ENOUGH ABUSED
Answer: What you might get from a SENATOR—"NO TEARS"

120. **Jumbles:** FUDGE VISTA UNCLAD ENTICE
Answer: Rather big for ballet these days—AUDIENCES

121. **Jumbles:** COVEY WHEAT TURKEY ZODIAC
Answer: What happened when the garbage truck overturned—IT "REEKED" HAVOC

122. **Jumbles:** BOOTY TWEAK PHYSIC JURIST
Answer: Why the cherry picker disliked his job—IT WAS THE PITS

123. **Jumbles:** CREEK ABBOT NAPKIN UNFOLD
Answer: What the bald produce peddler ended up with—A BAKED BEAN

124. **Jumbles:** FOIST NAIVE UPLIFT FOURTH
Answer: The egotistical beauty queen was—AN "I"-FOOL

125. **Jumbles:** ARRAY RABBI BANDIT LIMBER
Answer: Another name for this ornithologist—A BIRD BRAIN

126. **Jumbles:** FISHY OCTET FAIRLY RAGLAN
Answer: How the electrician's helper treated his work—"LIGHTLY"

127. **Jumbles:** BEGOT ROBOT BALLAD LEVITY
Answer: How the boxer became the camp—WITH A BIG BELT

128. **Jumbles:** USURP ANISE TWINGE HANSOM
Answer: What they called the birthday preparations—A "WRAP" SESSION

129. **Jumbles:** BERET KAPOK BEWARE MOSAIC
Answer: What the patrons of the restaurant became—"WAITERS"

130. **Jumbles:** SCARY ELITE MYRIAD CORNEA
Answer: In one year and out the other—CALENDARS

131. **Jumbles:** DUNCE POUCH ADDING ENSURE
Answer: All the clocks at the antique clock store were this—SECONDHAND

132. **Jumbles:** STUNK HOLLY VANISH BOXING
Answer: You can't play this in school—HOOKY

133. **Jumbles:** DOOZY PLUME BITTER VISUAL
Answer: The new math teacher was having—PROBLEMS

134. **Jumbles:** BLUNT YOKEL SPEEDY SHADOW
Answer: She thought the street vendor was—PUSHY

135. **Jumbles:** PROWL PURGE SEESAW CHANGE
Answer: What do you call a rabbit on the lawn?—A GRASS HOPPER

136. **Jumbles:** PRUNE UPPED PERMIT RESUME
Answer: When the math teacher ended the lesson, she—SUMMED IT UP

137. **Jumbles:** CEASE PIXEL INVEST STUDIO
Answer: The new employee at the bakery was—A CUTIE PIE

138. **Jumbles:** DIRTY KNELT BROKEN FATHOM
Answer: When developing a new armored military vehicle during World War One, they formed a—THINK TANK

139. **Jumbles:** MADLY FLUID PLURAL OXYGEN
Answer: A millionaire's dog's favorite place—
THE LAP OF LUXURY

140. **Jumbles:** HONOR FIGHT NAUSEA SMOOTH
Answer: Mommy knew something was wrong because Billy came—STRAIGHT HOME

141. **Jumbles:** BATCH MONEY FIGURE JOYFUL
Answer: When a lion is great at word puzzles, he's known as "King—OF THE JUMBLE"

142. **Jumbles:** JUROR LUNCH COMEDY SKINNY
Answer: After getting the bill for his truck's new suspension system, he was—SHOCKED

143. **Jumbles:** LIMIT QUASH HAGGLE SKIMPY
Answer: The mountaintop casino featured—HIGH STAKES

144. **Jumbles:** DRAFT HYENA SMOKER PULPIT
Answer: The finale of the bowling tournament was so exciting that you could—HEAR A PIN DROP

145. **Jumbles:** PLUMB THUMB ENTICE DRAGON
Answer: The Thanksgiving turkey was so good that everyone—GOBBLED IT UP

146. **Jumbles:** UPPED STASH SONATA SEESAW
Answer: The oceanography class consisted of—
"SEA" STUDENTS

147. **Jumbles:** QUALM LEVEL TANGLE MICRON
Answer: Basketball players enjoy away games because this is allowed—TRAVELING

148. **Jumbles:** ADAGE LEAVE FONDUE SYRUPY
Answer: With all the taxes and surcharges, gasoline is—
"FEE-YOU-L"

149. **Jumbles:** SWOON DEPTH PRANCE ABSURD
Answer: Picking up food can make it hard to—
DROP POUNDS

150. **Jumbles:** FACET SILKY TYRANT UNTOLD
Answer: Minnie Mouse was telling Mickey about her day, and Mickey was—ALL EARS

151. **Jumbles:** TWIRL CLASS HORRID TRUDGE
Answer: When they told them they'd be driving clockwise, the drivers said—ALL RIGHT

152. **Jumbles:** THUMB WOUND OBLONG FIRMLY
Answer: The dentist was happy to get the new patient as a result of—WORD OF MOUTH

153. **Jumbles:** STRUM ALIAS INDIGO INDOOR
Answer: When it came to Neil Armstrong's determination to walk on the moon, he was—ON A MISSION

154. **Jumbles:** LARVA STALL FIGURE NAUSEA
Answer: The fight at the family reunion was—ALL RELATIVE

155. **Jumbles:** BRAWN YEAST LESSON LIZARD
Answer: The pregnant woman would need to leave the cookout quickly…it was—LABOR DAY

156. **Jumbles:** VILLA COACH ANYHOW TENANT
Answer: The big cat finished the test quickly because he was a—"CHEAT-AH"

157. **Jumbles:** EXERT ONION UPROOT SUDDEN
Answer: He wanted to go out to lunch with his friends after the marathon, but he—NEEDED TO RUN

158. **Jumbles:** ELUDE JOINT AGENCY EASILY
Answer: The cyclops' son wanted an action figure for his birthday, so they bought him a—G-"EYE" JOE

159. **Jumbles:** WHIRL DUNCE LONGER WARMTH
Answer: Climbing the mountain was going fine until the weather—WENT DOWNHILL

160. **Jumbles:** STOOD PRISM NOVICE MARVEL
Answer: The arachnid had her legs examined by a doctor after becoming worried about her—SPIDER VEINS

161. **Jumbles:** UPSHOT REDUCE APIECE BRASSY AFFIRM MADMAN
Answer: What the doc's diagnosis was—A "RASH" DECISION

162. **Jumbles:** PURITY LAXITY MYOPIC CROUCH NOGGIN FETISH
Answer: What the skydivers used—A PAIR O' CHUTES

163. **Jumbles:** GASKET OPAQUE CURFEW BRIDLE UNHOLY OSSIFY
Answer: What the late-night drummer faced from his neighbors—"RE-PERCUSSIONS"

164. **Jumbles:** TOFFEE CODGER OUTBID BRANDY SLEIGH FINERY
Answer: What the workers considered their use of the company kitchen—A "FRIDGE" BENEFIT

165. **Jumbles:** JINGLE FEUDAL ROSARY ENTITY INVITE TEAPOT
Answer: There's always one—AGAINST THE TIED

166. **Jumbles:** UNCOIL INFLUX FROLIC JOYOUS TRIPLE MARTIN
Answer: What the homeowner sought when he bought earthquake insurance—A NO-"FAULT" POLICY

167. **Jumbles:** UNRULY HOTBED CALICO MARMOT QUORUM ACCORD
Answer: What the diners got when their meals arrived cold—HOT UNDER THE COLLAR

168. **Jumbles:** BARIUM NEEDLE COERCE UNTRUE FIDDLE ABSURD
Answer: What the eccentric tycoon left in his will—
A LOT TO BE "DESIRED"

169. **Jumbles:** VALUED BONNET GULLET AFRAID MASCOT FLAUNT
Answer: What the uptight librarian experienced when she drove a race car—LIFE IN THE FAST LANE

170. **Jumbles:** OUTBID LAUNCH CUDGEL APATHY FEMALE DETAIN
Answer: An angler either has fish lying about him, or he's—
LYING ABOUT THEM

171. **Jumbles:** HARDER DEVOUR POLICE ACCEPT SWAMPY INVERT
Answer: He told his wife there wouldn't be a line to see the movie, but he would—STAND CORRECTED

172. **Jumbles:** GALLON SPRUCE TIRADE ABSURD SCULPT HYPHEN
Answer: The middle of the mall was the—
SHOPPING CENTER

173. **Jumbles:** ALPACA BREACH DEFACE HIGHLY LOPPED REVERT
Answer: When the librarian gave her new employee instructions, she gave her an—ALPHABETICAL ORDER

174. **Jumbles:** HERMIT ACCEPT UTMOST QUARRY USEFUL INVERT
Answer: Her cat wanted a back rub, so she gave him one—
"PURR" HIS REQUEST

175. **Jumbles:** PROVEN IMPEDE UNTOLD WEALTH ASSURE SESAME
Answer: When Henry Ford's business expanded, it created the—"AUTO-MAN" EMPIRE

176. **Jumbles:** LOUNGE ROOKIE ANYWAY HINDER CAVITY AROUND
Answer: After the woman gave birth in the taxi, the driver told her there was—NO DELIVERY CHARGE

177. **Jumbles:** PARDON USEFUL TURNIP PLEDGE ACCENT DOCTOR
Answer: The farmer raised fruits and vegetables because he wanted to—PRODUCE PRODUCE

178. **Jumbles:** BROKER STUDIO PIGLET SPRAWL FIASCO UNSEEN
Answer: This time he was really going to quit smoking—
NO IFS, ANDS, OR "BUTTS"

179. **Jumbles:** BROTHER UPDATE FORGET ODDEST GAMBLE UNWIND
Answer: This maple tree would eventually provide shade in the summertime without a—SHADOW OF A DOUBT

180. **Jumbles:** EMERGE HYMNAL TEDIUM UPROAR INHALE TICKLE
Answer: Getting her son to the dentist was—
LIKE PULLING TEETH

Need More Jumbles®?

Order any of these books through your bookseller or call Triumph Books toll-free at 800-335-5323.

Jumble® Books

More than 175 puzzles each!

Cowboy Jumble®
$9.95 • ISBN: 978-1-62937-355-3

Jammin' Jumble®
$9.95 • ISBN: 1-57243-844-4

Java Jumble®
$9.95 • ISBN: 978-1-60078-415-6

Jazzy Jumble®
$9.95 • ISBN: 978-1-57243-962-7

Jet Set Jumble®
$9.95 • ISBN: 978-1-60078-353-1

Joyful Jumble®
$9.95 • ISBN: 978-1-60078-079-0

Juke Joint Jumble®
$9.95 • ISBN: 978-1-60078-295-4

Jumble® at Work
$9.95 • ISBN: 1-57243-147-4

Jumble® Celebration
$9.95 • ISBN: 978-1-60078-134-6

Jumble® Circus
$9.95 • ISBN: 978-1-60078-739-3

Jumble® Drag Race
$9.95 • ISBN: 978-1-63937-483-3

Jumble® Explorer
$9.95 • ISBN: 978-1-60078-854-3

Jumble® Explosion
$9.95 • ISBN: 978-1-60078-078-3

Jumble® Fever
$9.95 • ISBN: 1-57243-593-3

Jumble® Fiesta
$9.95 • ISBN: 1-57243-626-3

Jumble® Fun
$9.95 • ISBN: 1-57243-379-5

Jumble® Galaxy
$9.95 • ISBN: 978-1-60078-583-2

Jumble® Genius
$9.95 • ISBN: 1-57243-896-7

Jumble® Getaway
$9.95 • ISBN: 978-1-60078-547-4

Jumble® Gold
$9.95 • ISBN: 978-1-62937-354-6

Jumble® Grab Bag
$9.95 • ISBN: 1-57243-273-X

Jumble® Gymnastics
$9.95 • ISBN: 978-1-62937-306-5

Jumble® Jackpot
$9.95 • ISBN: 1-57243-897-5

Jumble® Jailbreak
$9.95 • ISBN: 978-1-62937-002-6

Jumble® Jambalaya
$9.95 • ISBN: 978-1-60078-294-7

Jumble® Jamboree
$9.95 • ISBN: 1-57243-696-4

Jumble® Jitterbug
$9.95 • ISBN: 978-1-60078-584-9

Jumble® Journey
$9.95 • ISBN: 978-1-62937-549-6

Jumble® Jubilee
$9.95 • ISBN: 1-57243-231-4

Jumble® Juggernaut
$9.95 • ISBN: 978-1-60078-026-4

Jumble® Junction
$9.95 • ISBN: 1-57243-380-9

Jumble® Jungle
$9.95 • ISBN: 978-1-57243-961-0

Jumble® Kingdom
$9.95 • ISBN: 1-62937-079-8

Jumble® Knockout
$9.95 • ISBN: 1-62937-078-1

Jumble® Madness
$9.95 • ISBN: 1-892049-24-4

Jumble® Magic
$9.95 • ISBN: 978-1-60078-795-9

Jumble® Marathon
$9.95 • ISBN: 978-1-62937-548-9

Jumble® Parachute
$9.95 • ISBN: 978-1-60078-944-1

Jumble® Safari
$9.95 • ISBN: 978-1-60078-675-4

Jumble® See & Search
$9.95 • ISBN: 1-57243-549-6

Jumble® See & Search 2
$9.95 • ISBN: 1-57243-734-0

Jumble® Sensation
$9.95 • ISBN: 978-1-60078-548-1

Jumble® Surprise
$9.95 • ISBN: 1-57243-320-5

Jumble® Symphony
$9.95 • ISBN: 978-1-62937-131-3

Jumble® Theater
$9.95 • ISBN: 978-1-63937-484-03

Jumble® University
$9.95 • ISBN: 978-1-62937-001-9

Jumble® Vacation
$9.95 • ISBN: 978-1-60078-796-6

Jumble® Wedding
$9.95 • ISBN: 978-1-62937-307-2

Jumble® Workout
$9.95 • ISBN: 978-1-60078-943-4

Jumpin' Jumble®
$9.95 • ISBN: 978-1-60078-027-1

Lunar Jumble®
$9.95 • ISBN: 978-1-60078-853-6

Monster Jumble®
$9.95 • ISBN: 978-1-62937-213-6

Mystic Jumble®
$9.95 • ISBN: 978-1-62937-130-6

Outer Space Jumble®
$9.95 • ISBN: 978-1-60078-416-3

Rainy Day Jumble®
$9.95 • ISBN: 978-1-60078-352-4

Ready, Set, Jumble®
$9.95 • ISBN: 978-1-60078-133-0

Rock 'n' Roll Jumble®
$9.95 • ISBN: 978-1-60078-674-7

Royal Jumble®
$9.95 • ISBN: 978-1-60078-738-6

Sports Jumble®
$9.95 • ISBN: 1-57243-113-X

Summer Fun Jumble®
$9.95 • ISBN: 1-57243-114-8

Touchdown Jumble®
$9.95 • ISBN: 978-1-62937-212-9

Travel Jumble®
$9.95 • ISBN: 1-57243-198-9

TV Jumble®
$9.95 • ISBN: 1-57243-461-9

Oversize Jumble® Books

More than 500 puzzles each!

Generous Jumble®
$19.95 • ISBN: 1-57243-385-X

Giant Jumble®
$19.95 • ISBN: 1-57243-349-3

Gigantic Jumble®
$19.95 • ISBN: 1-57243-426-0

Jumbo Jumble®
$19.95 • ISBN: 1-57243-314-0

The Very Best of Jumble® BrainBusters
$19.95 • ISBN: 1-57243-845-2

GENEROUS
JUMBLE
A BIG BOOK FOR BIG FANS
OVER 500
GIANT
JUMBLE
500

Jumble® Crosswords™

More than 175 puzzles each!

More Jumble® Crosswords™
$9.95 • ISBN: 1-57243-386-8

Jumble® Crosswords™ Jackpot
$9.95 • ISBN: 1-57243-615-8

Jumble® Crosswords™ Jamboree
$9.95 • ISBN: 1-57243-787-1

Jumble® BrainBusters™

More than 175 puzzles each!

Jumble® BrainBusters™
$9.95 • ISBN: 1-892049-28-7

Jumble® BrainBusters™ II
$9.95 • ISBN: 1-57243-424-4

Jumble® BrainBusters™ III
$9.95 • ISBN: 1-57243-463-5

Jumble® BrainBusters™ IV
$9.95 • ISBN: 1-57243-489-9

Jumble® BrainBusters™ 5
$9.95 • ISBN: 1-57243-548-8

Jumble® BrainBusters™ Bonanza
$9.95 • ISBN: 1-57243-616-6

Boggle™ BrainBusters™
$9.95 • ISBN: 1-57243-592-5

Boggle™ BrainBusters™ 2
$9.95 • ISBN: 1-57243-788-X

Jumble® BrainBusters™ Junior
$9.95 • ISBN: 1-892049-29-5

Jumble® BrainBusters™ Junior II
$9.95 • ISBN: 1-57243-425-2

Fun in the Sun with Jumble® BrainBusters™
$9.95 • ISBN: 1-57243-733-2

JUMBLE
BrainBusters
A Workout for Your M
JUMBLE
BrainBusters
5
Boggle
BrainBusters!
JUMBLE
BrainBusters!
IV
JUMBLE
BrainBusters
Junior
II